MASTER MENTAL TOUGHNESS
IN SOCCER

BY SIMON HARTLEY & DARREN LAVER

Printed by CreateSpace (An Amazon Company)

Coaches who work at all levels are becoming aware of the importance of players having "mental toughness", especially at an Elite level. This is something that coaches are paying lots of attention to and need a clear understanding of when developing players for the future. Darren Laver and Simon Hartley's book enables coaches to have a framework and a structure, to develop the psychology required in players and teams for the modern game. Lots has been written about the game in other aspects, like tactics and the technical ability. This book has a focus on the psychology of the game and the techniques to build Mental Toughness. This makes a big difference at the very top where lack of toughness has the potential to derail players from getting to the top of their profession. This book will help coaches deliver a program that allows the players to reach their full potential.

Paul Williams, 220 Appearances in the Premier League, Birmingham City - First team coach, Swansea FC - Assistant Manager (Assistant to Bob Bradley), Nottingham Forest - Head Coach, England U20s - Head Coach

Experienced coaches are fully capable of recognizing "mental toughness" when they see it. Laver and Hartley, in this incredible book, give the coach a specific plan, pathway and a program to develop that psycho -social aspect of the game in players and teams. Much has been written about the tactics and techniques associated with soccer. The difference at the very top level, however, in the mind, and this book provides the framework for you, the coach, to train players to create and maintain that winner's mindset.

Andy Poklad, Director of Coaching, Tennessee State Soccer Association

Mastering Mental Toughness is quite exceptional in the regard that it actually promotes and stimulates critical thinking, with the detail on just that: helping professional players understand how they can gain an advantage by creating a small percentile of difference mentally. That is what makes the difference at the top level. Often that is what separates the good and the great, particularly on the world stage. This unique insight promotes ways to enhance these skills and actually experience putting them to use in the sporting environment to make a difference.

Robin Shroot, Professional Soccer Player, Nashville Soccer Club, Birmingham City,
AFC Wimbledon

CONTENTS

Meet Simon & Darren.. 4

Introduction... 5

Stage Zero: Coaches Quiz... 7

Stage One: Understanding Mental Toughness... 9

Stage Two: Consistent Optimal Performance.. 19

Stage Three: Accountability and Responsibility....................................... 35

Stage Four: Entering The Discomfort Zone... 45

Stage Five: Toughness – Tenacity, Resilience and Composure........................... 59

Bibliography and Useful Links.. 73

About the Authors.. 78

MEET SIMON & DARREN

We go back a long way! To be honest, we go back more years than either of us like to admit.

We wanted to write a book that helps coaches and players to develop mental toughness. By writing this together, we can bring our various experiences and areas of expertise into one book. It means that you get the knowledge, insights and experience of two authors, not just one. However, we also know it could be a little confusing. As you're reading, you may be wondering which one of us is talking. So, to help, we've added these very accurate, almost picture-perfect portraits, to help.

Here's how it works...

I'm Simon Hartley. My background is sport psychology. For a little over 20 years, I've had the pleasure of coaching some of the greatest athletes and sports teams in the world, including world champions, world record holders, Olympians and championship winning teams. I've also worked in the English Premier League and in International Football.

I have also been studying world class performers, teams, leaders and organizations, to understand what differentiates them from the rest. Around 10 years ago, I founded Be World Class, to help people adopt these principles to become great too.

I'm Darren Laver. I am the director and founder of The International Street Soccer Association (ISSA) and the Virtual Director of Coaching (The VDOC), a soccer club consultancy organization. I am a sport scientist, author and a globally recognized coach and exhibition performer.

I have dedicated my life to coaching players to improve their creative skills. I provide training programs, expert advice, coach education for amateur and professional clubs, governing associations, councils and communities across the world. I also work as a 'Technical Consultant' for the Tennessee State Soccer Association.

We've been developing Mental Toughness in athletes and players for decades. The methods and tools within this book work… time and again… at the very highest level of sport. We are excited to share them with you and we genuinely hope that you gain as much benefit from them as we have!

INTRODUCTION:
WELCOME TO MASTER MENTAL TOUGHNESS IN SOCCER

What is mental toughness?

It's something you might notice, as a coach, We see the absence of it when we watch our star player collapsing under pressure or when we see our team freezing; like rabbits in the headlights. It is the kind of quality that will separate the truly great soccer players from the also-runs.

This book is designed to help you not only understand what mental toughness is, but also to find ways of building it in yourself and the players you are coaching. It does not attempt to cover everything about mental toughness. Instead, it is an introductory framework that gives you tips which you can explore and build upon.

What is Covered in This Book?

DEFINITION OF MENTAL TOUGHNESS: We will define what mental toughness is, and what it is not. More importantly, we'll start to understand when we're seeing true mental toughness and when we're not. Players who beat their chests and shout a lot are often not displaying mental toughness at all. We will get under the skin and beyond the dictionary definitions. If we want to coach mental toughness, we need to know what it looks like, sounds like, thinks like and behaves like. And, we need to understand it from the perspectives of both players and coaches. Once we understand what mental toughness really is, we can start to develop it.

STAGES OF MENTAL TOUGHNESS: This book will give you a step-by-step process to build mental strength. This not only gives you the theory, but also a practical way to translate it into on-field performance.

The five stages are:

Stage 1 – Understanding Mental Toughness

Stage 2 – Consistent Optimal Performance

Stage 3 – Accountability and Responsibility

Stage 4 – Entering "The Discomfort Zone"

Stage 5 – Toughness, Resilience, Tenacity and Composure

KEY LESSONS: This book is a practical guide. Our aim is to give you strategies, methods, and tools that you can take away and use in your coaching. The Key Lessons section helps you understand how to apply the principles and ideas that we will explore. It is a chance for you to reflect on how to use this knowledge in your coaching, with your players.

Let us begin with a quiz. This will help us to start developing a highly practical understanding of mental toughness. We have called this "stage zero" for an important reason: this is the beginning. It helps us to identify both the start point in our journey and the destination. It also provides us with some very valuable awareness: a critical ingredient in this process!

Your answers will start to highlight which elements of mental toughness you may already have, and those you need to work on. Once we know this, you can start getting to work!

As Sir Edmund Hillary once said:

"It is not the mountain we conquer but ourselves".

STAGE ZERO: COACHES QUIZ

This is not a test. We are not trying to find out whether an expert on mental strength or even soccer. What we are looking for very specific things that will help you gain as much as possible from this book. No-one is marking or assessing you and, as the authors, we will never read your answers. This is your quiz and the answers belong to you. The purpose is to help you gain a deeper understanding of yourself and mental toughness.

Take time to reflect on the following questions:

a) Your Knowledge: What do you know about mental toughness? What more do you want to know? How are you going to build on your current knowledge?

b) Your Attitudes: What are your attitudes about mental toughness? Do you think it is something positive or negative? Do you aspire to it or do you fear it? What do you think about people who are mentally tough or even mental weak? Do you admire them, do you despise them, pity them, or even feel repelled by them?

c) Your Perceptions: Can you identify those people who display mental toughness? Are you able to see those who do not have mental toughness? What are the most important indicators for you when you are deciding whether someone is mentally tough or not? What does this mean for you in terms of your own practice and behavior?

d) Your Behavior: What do you do that shows mental strength? What do you do that shows mental weaknesses? When are you most comfortable? When are you least comfortable? What parts of your persona and personality do you most want to change? How can you change it? Does this affect the way in which you coach? How does it change it? What impact does this have on your players?

e) SWOT Analysis: What are your strengths? What are your weaknesses? What are your opportunities in the game? What are your threats in the game and profession? How can you use your strengths in order to overcome your weaknesses? How can you use your opportunities in order to overcome the threats that you are facing?

The aim is to ensure that you know what you are good at, what you would like to be good at, and how you get there. Have a go at these:

Mental Toughness Quiz for Coaches

Answer these questions. There is no right or wrong. Take your time. Write down the answers. Read them back and reflect on them.

1. Who are the first names on your team-sheet?
2. Why have you chosen those players?
3. What have they got that others do not have?
4. Who are your best leaders on the team?
5. Who gets you out of trouble?
6. Who drives the team on?
7. Who steps up when the team needs them to?
8. When you look at the very best players you have coached, what separates them from the rest?
9. What do they have that others don't have?
10. If you had to identify one player who could make it at the very highest level, who would it be?
11. What do they have, which the others don't?
12. What do you think about talent? Is it enough to be successful?
13. What do players need in addition to talent?
14. What do you consider to be a good attitude in soccer?
15. How do you know whether or not a player has a good attitude?
16. What mindset helps you win games?
17. What mindset makes you lose games?
18. What kind of character do you need to be successful in professional soccer?
19. Which players you consider to be mentally tough? List their names.
20. Which qualities make them mentally tough? List these qualities.
21. List players who you do not consider to be mentally tough.
22. What shows that they are not mentally tough?
23. What would you do to make these players mentally tough? Describe every step of the process.
24. Would you describe yourself as mentally tough or mentally weak at the moment?
25. Can you give detailed reasons why you described yourself that way?

What does this tell you about...?

a. Yourself
b. Your mental toughness
c. Your players
d. Their mental toughness
e. Your coaching
f. How you coach toughness in your players

Now that you have completed the quiz, it is time to move to Stage One.

STAGE ONE: UNDERSTANDING MENTAL TOUGHNESS

Welcome to Stage One.

During this section, we're going to answer a several questions:

1. What is mental toughness?
2. What does mental toughness look like and sound like in action?
3. What are the effects of mental toughness on the players and the game?
4. How does mental toughness change a player?
5. What can mental toughness give you, the coach, and the players you are coaching?

Stage One is our foundation. As with anything, a strong foundation is ultimately critical to our success.

The first stage will help you to develop a clear picture of Mental Toughness. It is very difficult to build something if we don't fully understand it. Imagine how much more difficult it would be to build a jigsaw puzzle if someone took away the picture on the front of the box.

Once we have a good understanding of what Mental Toughness is - how it looks, sounds, thinks and acts - we can begin to cultivate it in our players. The whole Five-Stage process looks like this:

Stage 1 – Understanding Mental Toughness (You are here)
Stage 2 – Consistent Optimal Performance
Stage 3 – Accountability and Responsibility
Stage 4 – Enter The Discomfort Zone
Stage 5 – Toughness: Tenacity, Resilience and Composure

As you can see, each stage acts as a foundation for the next. Therefore, we need to work through them, one step at a time.

During this stage, you will learn:

What Mental Toughness is, and what it is not!
How to recognize Mental Toughness in your players.
The 5 Key traits of Mental Toughness and how to spot them.
How to assess the Mental Toughness of your players using the Mental Toughness Matrix.
What you will see and hear as your players become tougher.

We will also share a valuable tool: *The Mental Toughness Matrix*

Off we go!

Why Do We Need Mental Toughness?

Arguably, to be successful, we need a healthy dose of Mental Toughness. I have seen first-hand evidence of its importance in my own work with world-class athletes. Whilst researching my second book, How to Shine,[1] I also interviewed world-class performers in a diverse range of disciplines outside of sport to find out what differentiates them from their peers. It seems Mental Toughness is a key factor in the success of a four-time Michelin starred chef, a world-class mountaineer, a world barista champion, a record breaking polar explorer, the head of a world-renowned science organization, and special forces personnel.

Mental Toughness allows these people to push themselves and extend their limits. It enables them to thrive in adversity. Their Mental Toughness drives them to take on those challenges that their peers back away from. It allows them to constantly improve their performance by trying and failing! Perhaps more importantly, it also enables them to ask those uncomfortable, searching, questions and find the difficult answers.

If we wish to develop mentally tough athletes, it makes sense to begin by understanding what Mental Toughness is and what it is not!

What Is Mental Toughness?

Sport psychology researcher, Dr. Michael Sheard,[2] has investigated the phenomenon we call 'Mental Toughness'. He also acknowledges its importance in the success of athletes and sports teams. In fact, Dr. Sheard describes it as "the stuff of champions" (p.7); it is courage to stand tall in the face of adversity; and refuse to be intimidated.

Jon Hammermeister[3] (a performance psychologist from the US Army) recognizes that some of the skills associated with Mental Toughness include the ability to:

- Be self-motivated
- Maintain confidence
- Focus under pressure
- Be in control of emotions
- Consistently perform close to one's potential.

While that's useful information, it doesn't necessarily help us to identify mentally tough individuals when we see them. To make it more real...

- How would you know a mentally tough athlete if you saw one?
- What traits would they exhibit?
- What characteristics would you see?
- How would they behave?
- What would they say?

In my work as a sport psychology consultant and performance coach, I have been fascinated by the concept of Mental Toughness. I have seen many athletes and teams who have crumbled when they've hit tough challenges. Some teams imploded at crucial times during a game, or during a season. Some panicked when they went behind. They seemed to throw their game plan out of the window when they were questioned.

For many years, I defined Mental Toughness as the ability to stick to the game plan - no matter what! Obviously, 'the game plan' needs to be flexible and adaptable. However, I would argue that we should not abandon it completely and start panicking at the first sign of trouble.

I have also seen many athletes who seem to shrivel up when they're exposed to criticism. It is hard for some to take, especially if that criticism is very vocal and comes from 40,000 fans on a Saturday afternoon. In fact, whilst working in an English Premier League football club a number of years ago, our coaching staff developed a saying:

"When the going gets tough, the tough hide under the treatment table".

We used to see the number of injuries rise (and take longer to heal) when the team was struggling, and the players were being booed by the fans. The players were actually using the treatment room to escape! Coincidently, the captain (who did the shouting and fist waving) was the most regular visitor to the treatment room if we lost at home. Interestingly, our problem wasn't bruised bodies; it was bruised egos.

Mental Toughness Clues

Michael Sheard[2] identifies a number of traits that he associates with mentally tough athletes:

- A winning mentality
- Work ethic
- Self-confidence
- Motivation
- Attitude control
- Positive energy

When we look at athletes, we notice a group of traits that inform us about their Mental Toughness including:

1. Athletes who consistently perform at their best in adverse conditions:
   Mentally tough athletes tend to be focused, confident and motivated, whatever the situation. Every athlete experiences their peaks and troughs, whether that is through injury, lack of form, de-selection, a run of poor results, or whatever. Every athlete has been in situations where the chips are down, and they have their backs to the wall. Mentally tough athletes tend to apply themselves consistently, whether they are on a high, or at the bottom of the deepest low. I often say to athletes, *"I want to know what you're like on the shitty days"*.

2. Athletes who come back stronger from set-backs:

Athletes with mental strength tend to display 'bounce-back ability'. I have come to realize that great athletes seem to experience the same amount of 'good luck' and 'bad luck' as everyone else. However, their response to their 'luck' is normally different. When they experience set-backs, mentally tough athletes knuckle down, apply themselves, learn as much as they possibly can from the experience and grow from it.

3. Athletes who are composed in 'pressurized situations':

When athletes perceive that they are under pressure, some will panic. Sometimes the game plan flies out of the window and they start to make strange decisions and unforced errors. Mentally tough athletes, however, tend to have the ability to remain composed. They tend not to panic, they stay on task, keep focused and stick to the game plan. When they make mistakes, they simply focus back onto the task in hand and execute their skills.

4. Athletes who actively seek out, and thrive in, their Discomfort Zone:

Some athletes will respond well if they are pushed outside of their comfort zones. Truly great athletes go a step further. They actively seek out opportunities to push themselves into their Discomfort Zone. The world-class athletes that I've worked with will say that the alarm bells start ringing when they become comfortable. These people relish the challenge and go looking for it!

5. Athletes who push to their limit, not just the point of discomfort:

Most people stop when things become uncomfortable. Although we think of this in a physical sense (i.e. the point we become tired or feel physical pain), this concept extends to other limits too. Some people give up when they've tried a new skill a few times and it's not worked perfectly. They don't like the feeling of 'failing' because it is uncomfortable. Other people keep going and keep failing, until they get it right. They don't stop at the point where it becomes uncomfortable, they stop when they hit their limit.

6. Athletes who are self-critical and seek critical feedback from others:

Some athletes are uncomfortable with criticism. Others will listen, take criticism on board and acknowledge it. The better athletes will recognize that it is a gift and use it to its fullest extent. The world-class athletes that I've met actually seek out critical feedback and then squeeze every possible ounce of benefit from it. To them, critical feedback is like oxygen. It fuels their development. Without it they know they cannot grow.

Extreme Mental Toughness

Over the years, I have witnessed many athletes and teams who displayed incredible Mental Toughness. I worked with incredibly tough individuals, such as mountaineers, polar explorers, adventure racers, extreme athletes and special-forces personnel. These people conquer some phenomenal challenges.

Mountaineer Alan Hinkes is one of around a dozen people who have reached the summit of all 14 of the world's 8000+ meter peaks. On one occasion, he found himself in a nightmare situation at the peak of the world's third highest mountain.

He was 8500 meters above sea level, on his own, in the dark and in the middle of a blizzard. In his words, he thought he was going to die. His own Mental Toughness allowed him to focus and get himself off the mountain.

Polar explorer Ben Saunders has faced similar dangers in his solo treks in the Arctic when exhausted, starving hungry, frost-bitten and under attack from a polar bear.

World record breaking ultra-distance runner Andy McMenemy completed 66 ultra-marathons in 66 days after injuring his Achilles tendon on day two and being admitted to hospital on day twenty-six with a suspected fractured shin. He got up on day twenty-seven and ran an ultra-marathon.

Adventure racer Bruce Duncan has overcome injuries, lack of sleep and hyperthermia to complete his mammoth 6-7 day races.

These are all extreme displays of Mental Toughness!

In fact, after watching some truly tough people and listening to their stories, I extended my definition of Mental Toughness:

"the ability to keep going and not give up, even when every fiber of your being screams at you to stop".

But not all of us will be at the top of 8,000m high mountains, or crossing the Arctic Ocean, or running through a gun battle. So how can we see toughness outside of those extreme conditions? Is the tough individual the loudest? Are they the ones who run out of the dressing room screaming? Are they the one who is most physically dominant? Or... are they the ones who will push themselves the hardest? Are they the athletes that are willing to enter their discomfort zone? Are they the people that will venture into the unknown and take on new challenges? Perhaps, the tough athletes are the ones that take complete responsibility for their performance at all times.

Mentally Tough Athletes

In 2006, I worked with a Team GB Olympic swimmer called Chris Cook, as he prepared for the final of a major world event. He was waiting in the 'call room' with the other seven finalists. One of them, an Australian, came up to Chris and rubbed his knuckle on Chris' head. He started trying to intimidate Chris verbally and physically, in an attempt undermine Chris' confidence. Chris sat, looked at him and smiled. He didn't say a word in response because he didn't need to.

Chris knew that the Australian was in trouble. Why did the Australian feel the need to intimidate Chris? Did he not think he could win the race on his own merit? Did he have to pull Chris back, in order to stand a chance of beating him? Interestingly, Dr. Michael Sheard[2] referred to 'a refusal to be intimidated', in his description of Mental Toughness. This is not the same as feeling the need to intimidate others!

Sometimes fear can be dressed up as toughness. Bravado tends to be a façade: a form of 'fake toughness'. In fact, I would suggest that bravado is often a sign of weakness rather than strength.

Chris knew that his job was simple. He had to swim two lengths of that swimming pool as quickly as he could. He'd worked incredibly hard in training and could not have been better prepared. He'd overcome considerable adversity to get there, which gave him a deep sense of confidence in his own ability. All he had to do now was to swim two lengths of the pool. If Chris swam quicker than everyone else, he'd win. If someone else swam faster than him, they'd win. Chris knew if he simply swam as quickly as he could, he'd done his job. It doesn't get any more complicated than that.

If we want to know what Mental Toughness looks like, we can learn a lot from this example. The tough athlete is not the one trying to dominate or intimidate his opponent. The tougher of the two is the one who sat calmly, smiled and looked his opponent in the eye. He's also the one that remained completely focused on his job, and refused to be distracted from it. I doubt you'll be surprised when I tell you that Chris won the Gold Medal that day!

This is all very well, but it doesn't answer the burning question...

How Do We Develop Mental Toughness?

Often Mental Toughness develops almost by chance. Athletes can become tough as a result of their environment. Sometimes they are in an environment that is intensely competitive. In order to thrive and survive in those surroundings, they develop toughness. Through his studies of the world's sporting 'Gold Mines', Rasmus Ankersen[4] noted that in many cases, fierce competition gives rise to mentally tough athletes.

In order to succeed in the incredibly competitive environment, athletes are forced to become tough. If you want to become a successful female golfer in South Korea, or a world-class female tennis player in Russia, or a distance-runner in Kenya, you have to be tough enough to beat the thousands of others hoping to pip you to the dream. In Rasmus' words, there is a tiny percentage who 'pass through the eye of the needle'. The intensity of the training and competition dictates that only the toughest will make it.

In Jamaica, promising athletes attend the school athletics championships, known as The Champs. It is designed to be a 'high pressure' cauldron for the young athletes. The Champs is the focus of the entire nation. The stadium is packed with 30,000 people. It is on television and on the radio. Everyone is watching.

The thinking is simple. If a junior athlete can perform at The Champs, he or she will probably be able to perform anywhere.

However, we cannot rely on the world around us to make us tough. It is rare that athletes will find themselves in an extreme environment that demands Mental Toughness for them to succeed. Therefore, as coaches, we need to know how to cultivate it.

Mental Toughness should not be left to chance. This program provides the tools and resources to help you develop Mental Toughness deliberately and intentionally.

Master Mental Toughness is a Five Stage program. Think of it like stairs in a staircase. Each of the stages needs to be understood and mastered because it underpins the next.

We're at the start of Stage 1 – Understanding Mental Toughness. The first stage of the process is to develop a clear picture of Mental Toughness. It answers these questions:

- What does it look like?
- What does it sound like?
- What does it think like?
- What does it act like?
- Can we recognize it when we see it?
- Can we detect the subtle signs that tell us our players are becoming tougher?

Simply understanding what toughness looks like can help us to develop it.

Here's a tool that might help.

It's called, *The Mental Toughness Matrix*. I've used *The Mental Toughness Matrix* to help assess and develop toughness in elite and professional sport, education, the military and the world of business...

Mental Toughness Matrix

The Mental Toughness Matrix helps us assess toughnessw according to six key characteristics. For each of the characteristics, it also helps us understand what we might see and hear from people who are "tough", "not so tough" and three points in between.

Characteristic	Not So Tough				Tough
Consistency in Adverse Conditions	Can be significantly affected by relatively small adverse events.	Performance can be affected by relatively minor adverse conditions but the fluctuation is less significant.	Resistant to the more minor adverse conditions, but can be affected by moderate or more extreme situations.	Performance is generally stable, but can be affected by extreme adversity. However, performance swings are likely to be smaller.	Maintains focus & consistently delivers the processes with high quality execution in any situation.
Response to Set-Backs	Tends to experience significant knocks when they encounter set-backs. Normally emerges weaker as a result. Set-backs can be catastrophic.	Set-backs tend to leave 'scars'. Normally, the player does not return from the event as strongly. They tend to view set-backs as negative.	Tends not to be knocked by set-backs and normally comes back to a point of parity from any event.	Can gain from and learn from set-backs, finding opportunities that can give them some advantage.	Uses set-backs as an opportunity to strengthen. As a result they consistently emerge stronger from an event.
Composure Under Pressure	Often perceives 'pressure' in a situation and tends to crumble – makes strange decisions, abandons the game plan, panics and makes significant errors.	Becomes erratic and prone to errors when situations turn against them or if they perceive they are 'under pressure'.	Can become erratic or prone to errors in situations that they perceive to be 'highly pressurized'.	May become slightly more conservative, or take more risks in situations they perceive as 'highly pressurized'.	Consistent in their decision making, adherence to the game plan, focus, and execution, in any situation.

Characteristic	Not So Tough				Tough
Appetite for Discomfort Zone	Actively avoids their discomfort zone and consciously backs away from challenges that push them	Will occasionally enter their discomfort zone for short periods if the situation demands.	Will push into their discomfort zone when the need demands; but will normally only remain there as long as the demand remains.	Will choose to operate on the edge of their comfort / discomfort zone regularly, and take more significant strides into discomfort occasionally.	Actively seeks opportunities to take significant steps into their discomfort zone.
Willingness to Push To The Limit	Tends to give up before things become	Normally gives up at the point of mild discomfort or early experiences of discomfort.	Will endure discomfort on a needs basis, but tends not to endure significant discomfort for extended periods.	Will endure significant discomfort for extended periods and operate close to their true limits.	Will push it until breaking point so that they know the true limit, and then operate very close to the limit regularly.
Perception of Critical Feedback	Struggles to accept criticism and tends to ignore it.	Will accept some critical feedback, often	Accepts critical feedback comfortably and often uses it.	Readily accepts and uses critical feedback regularly, and views it as an opportunity to improve.	Actively seeks critical feedback, is proactively self-critical and works to get the maximum benefit from it.

Figure 1: The Mental Toughness Matrix

Importantly, **The Mental Toughness Matrix** also shows the journey from "not so tough" to "tough"; from left to right through the Matrix. These are the changes we see and hear as our athletes become tougher.

Summarizing Stage One

Congratulations. You're on your way to becoming a Mental Toughness Master!

Now that you've completed Stage One, you will understand the following:

1. What Mental Toughness is and what it is not!
   - ✓ i.e. the difference between genuine toughness and fake toughness.
2. How to recognize Mental Toughness in your players.
   - ✓ i.e. know when you do see signs of toughness, and don't see them.
3. The key traits of Mental Toughness and how to spot them.
   - ✓ Athletes who consistently perform at their best in adverse conditions
   - ✓ Athletes who come back stronger from set-backs
   - ✓ Athletes who are composed in 'pressurized situations'
   - ✓ Athletes who actively seek out, and thrive in, their Discomfort Zone
   - ✓ Athletes who push to their limit, not just the point of discomfort
   - ✓ Athletes who are self-critical and seek critical feedback from others
4. How to assess the Mental Toughness of your players using the Mental Toughness Matrix.
   - ✓ i.e. whether they are closer to 'tough' or 'not so tough'
5. What you will see and hear as your players become tougher.
   - ✓ i.e. you can use the Mental Toughness Matrix to identify the next steps in the development of your players.

Now that you know what mental toughness is, we can explore how you can begin to develop it in yourself and your players.

The Next Step...

Stage 2 – Consistent Optimal Performance

The ability to consistently perform at your best is one of the foundation stones of Mental Toughness. Fundamentally, players need to be able to take complete control over their thoughts and feelings. They need to be able to master and control their focus, confidence, and motivation. These skills will underpin their ability to perform under 'pressure'.

During Stage 2, you will learn how to coach your players to hone their focus, control their confidence, master their motivation and de-construct pressure. These are the essential ingredients of a strong mental game.

Are you ready to get going?

STAGE TWO: CONSISTENT OPTIMAL PERFORMANCE

What's the difference between your best performance, and your worst performance? Many people find that their performance fluctuates wildly from their best day to their worst. However, the very best performers find a way to perform close to their best in any situation; sometimes within just a couple of percentage points. How do they do that?

During Stage Two, we will discover how you perform at your best, consistently.

a. Maximizing Performance: How do you maximize your performance and that of your players? How do you ensure that you are always performing at the highest levels?

b. Confidence: How do you control your confidence to be able to perform in unfamiliar or difficult situations? How do you avoid over-confidence and yet perform well?

c. Motivation: How do you identify and build your own motivation as well as that of the players you are coaching? How do you ensure that you maintain consistent motivation in tough times?

d. Focus: How do you ensure that you focus on the right things at the right time? How do you cut out the distractions and focus on what really matters?

e. Pressure: Do you know what pressure is? How do you respond when you feel under-pressure?

f. Feelings: Do you have a handle on your feelings? How can you control your emotions so that they do not interfere with your performance?

g. Thoughts: Can you control the conversation between your ears? Can you engineer your headspace and create a mindset that helps your performance, not hinders it?

Welcome to Stage Two – Consistent Optimal Performance

Often Mental Toughness develops almost by chance. Athletes can become tough as a result of their environment. Sometimes they are in an environment that is intensely competitive. In order to thrive and survive in those surroundings, they develop toughness. Through his studies of the world's sporting 'Gold Mines', Rasmus Ankersen4 noted that in many cases fierce competition gives rise to mentally tough athletes.

Congratulations on completing Stage One. You may remember that the Master Mental Toughness program consists of Five Stages. Each stage underpins the next; a bit like a staircase.

The first stage helped you to develop a clear picture of Mental Toughness.

Stage 1 – Understanding Mental Toughness (Complete)
Stage 2 – Consistent Optimal Performance (You are here)
Stage 3 – Accountability & Responsibility
Stage 4 – Enter The Discomfort Zone
Stage 5 – Toughness: Tenacity, Resilience and Composure.

Stage Two will help you coach a solid mental game with your team.

Why Is This Stage So Important?

If we look back at what Mental Toughness is, we see phrases like….

"the ability to be self-motivated"
"maintain confidence and focus under pressure"
"be in control of emotions"
"consistently perform close to our potential"

It stands to reason that any athlete, who wants to maintain confidence under pressure, must first be able to control their own confidence. Equally, if we wish to remain focused under pressure, arguably we need to know how to hone our focus. In order to consistently perform close to our potential, we need to know how to engineer our mind and emotions to give us consistent optimal performance.

Whenever we look at the requirements of Mental Toughness, or indeed the requirements of a great mental game, we see the same key components:

- Focus
- Confidence
- Motivation

These three elements are the key to developing a great mental game, and ultimately to developing Mental Toughness.

What you will learn during this stage

This stage offers you the opportunity to learn the following:
1. How to consistently engineer a solid mental game in your players.
2. How to help your players to hone their focus.
3. How to coach players to control their confidence.
4. How to assist your players to master their motivation.
5. How to coach your players to de-construct 'pressure'.

Performing in Adversity

You may remember that "Consistency in Adverse Conditions" is one of the key elements in the *Mental Toughness Matrix*. It also shows what we're likely to see and hear from players who are "not so tough" (on the left hand side) to "tough" (right hand side). "Not so tough" players are vulnerable to distractions while the tougher players are completely focused on the task at hand and able to consistently deliver; regardless of the situation. It also shows there is a journey, from left to right. Therefore, we can develop from "not so tough" to "tough", by following this path.

Consistency in Advesere Conditions	Can be significantly affected by relatively small adverse events. Performance tend to follow changes in the situation.	Performance can be affected by relatively minor adverse conditions but the fluctuation is less significant.	Resistance to the more minor adverse conditions, but can be affected by moderate or more extreme situations.	Performance is generally stable, but can be affected by extreme adversity. However, performance swings are likely to be smaller.	Maintains focus, consistently delivers the processes with high quality execution in any situation.

Figure 2: Consistency in Adverse Conditions

So, what do you do in order to become consistent in your sport and activities as a coach? Consistency refers to the ability to perform at your best, regardless of the situation. It is one of the foundation stones of Mental Toughness. Fundamentally, players need to be able to take complete control over their thoughts and feelings. Athletes need to be able to master and control their focus, confidence and motivation. These skills also underpin their ability to perform under 'pressure'.

During Stage 2, you will learn how to coach your players to hone their focus, control their confidence, master their motivation and de-construct pressure. These are the essential ingredients of a strong mental game.

Are you ready to get cracking?

Workings of the Human Mind

Several years ago, I was working with a group of senior partners in a highly prestigious UK business, helping them too maximize their personal performance and the performance of the people around them.

During one of the sessions I was asked:

"So, which is most important then, confidence, motivation or focus?"

To be honest, I had never been asked the question before, so I had to stop and think for a minute. My brain tends to work in pictures and images. The image that entered my mind was that of a Formula One (F1) car. I explained that there are many key components in the car, all of which depend on each other. Having one on its own will not win you the race. It is the same with our mind. Crucially, confidence, motivation and focus work together. The F1 car as a fantastic analogy for this.

Imagine the F1 car. It has an incredibly powerful and finely tuned engine. It's perfectly obvious to most of us that in order to produce the immense speeds required to win a race, you need a powerful engine. However, a powerful engine alone will not win the race. A Dragster has a powerful engine, but it would not win the Monaco Grand Prix. Power is not the only quality that the car needs to possess. In order to win a race, our F1 car also requires maneuverability.

Formula One races are not run on straight tracks. Therefore, F1 cars need to have a state-of-the-art steering system in order to successfully navigate the course at high speed. As we all know, even these two components are not enough to win. In fact, even if we went through every nut and bolt in the car, we would still not find all the components required. In order to win a race, we need elements that lie outside the body of the car as well. Probably the most obvious is the driver. Arguably, the driver is one of the most vital factors in the success of our F1 car. If we had the best engine on earth, the number one steering system and the finest nuts and bolts money could buy, we wouldn't win the race with a timid driver who got scared driving over 30 mph.

All this talk of F1 cars is all well and good, but how does it relate to our trio of confidence, motivation and focus? This is how I see it:

1. **Motivation** is the engine. It is sometimes known as `drive'. It will provide us with the power and energy that we need.

2. **Focus** is our steering system. Motivation alone is not enough. If our motivation is undirected, we won't achieve our goals. It is very easy to be a motivated, energetic fool who runs around doing all sorts of interesting things that never produce an outcome. I suspect this is something we are all guilty of occasionally.

3. **Confidence** is our driver. Will the driver push himself and the car to the limits of its capacity, or back off a little at the crucial moments? Will the driver have enough confidence in the game plan to bide his time and only strike at exactly the right moment, or will he force a move that isn't there and spin off? Can the driver hold his nerve at crucial points in the race, or will he crack?

Maybe that's a long-winded way of saying you need all three. However, in reality it is a lot more than that. It shows that these three elements are dependent on each other and that there is an interaction between the three components. They all impact on each other. If they were colors, they would merge together as a spectrum rather than being individual blobs on a page.

If we look at the relationship between the three more closely, it's actually possible to see how they affect each other. When we have a simple, clear job, we have a very good chance of doing that job well[5,6]. Obviously, we also need to have the knowledge, skills, resources and desire to do it. But, having a simple, clear task initially gives us a massive advantage.

There is a huge amount of evidence for this, from a wide range of disciplines.

Task and Role Clarity

Researchers in management settings have identified that both task clarity[7] and role clarity[8],[9] have a significant impact on performance. When we understand the job, we're able to do it well. When we do the job well, we normally get a sense of satisfaction and fulfilment. Typically, as human beings, we like exhibiting mastery and we like to be successful in the things we do. So, when we perform well at something, we tend to want to do it again[10].

Psychologists such as Albert Bandura[11] have identified strong links between mastery, confidence, achievement and motivation. These links set up a positive spiral, which forms the foundation of our mental game:

- When I am focused on a simple, clear job, I give myself the best chance of being successful.
- When I have done the job well, I become confident and enjoy doing it.
- When I am confident in doing something, I am motivated to do it again.

These statements may seem perfectly obvious, but unfortunately their significance is often overlooked. Even some very well-qualified and experienced coaches have been unable to recognize the importance of these fundamental principles. They wonder why they have players who seem unmotivated, but they don't look for the reasons why. If someone is not confident in his or her ability to do the job, well, they might well shy away from it.

Think about those tasks that you always seem to put off:
- Do they tend to be tasks that you would consider easy and straightforward?
- Are they tasks that you're confident in, or are they the ones you are not sure about?
- Do they tend to be the tasks you are familiar with, or the ones you would describe as being more difficult or tricky?

The *positive spiral* that we have described also shows us how we can turn around under performance or deteriorating performance (such as the one we looked at in the Introduction). It tells us that focus is often the best starting point. Most people would probably think that a lack of confidence might best be addressed head on. I suspect you've have seen many football managers and coaches who believe that a pep talk is a good solution to a team's lack of confidence.

Many people believe that giving someone a pep talk or increasing the amount of positive feedback they receive will help to boost their confidence. Equally, many people would probably think that an inspirational speech or a set of attractive incentives would boost motivation. Although it seems logical on one level, in reality, they don't often have that effect. It does work in the movies – you know, those famous speeches in history such as the *Independence Day* Speech or the "Inches" speech in *Any Given Sunday*. They are iconic but also rare in our daily life. You might go through your lifetime without ever really experiencing a great speech being given.

Pep talks tend not to be the solution. In reality, they rarely have a significant or sustained effect on performance.

Research on performance spirals also indicates that verbal encouragement is not often enough to increase confidence or turn around a deteriorating performance[7].

The Positive Spiral

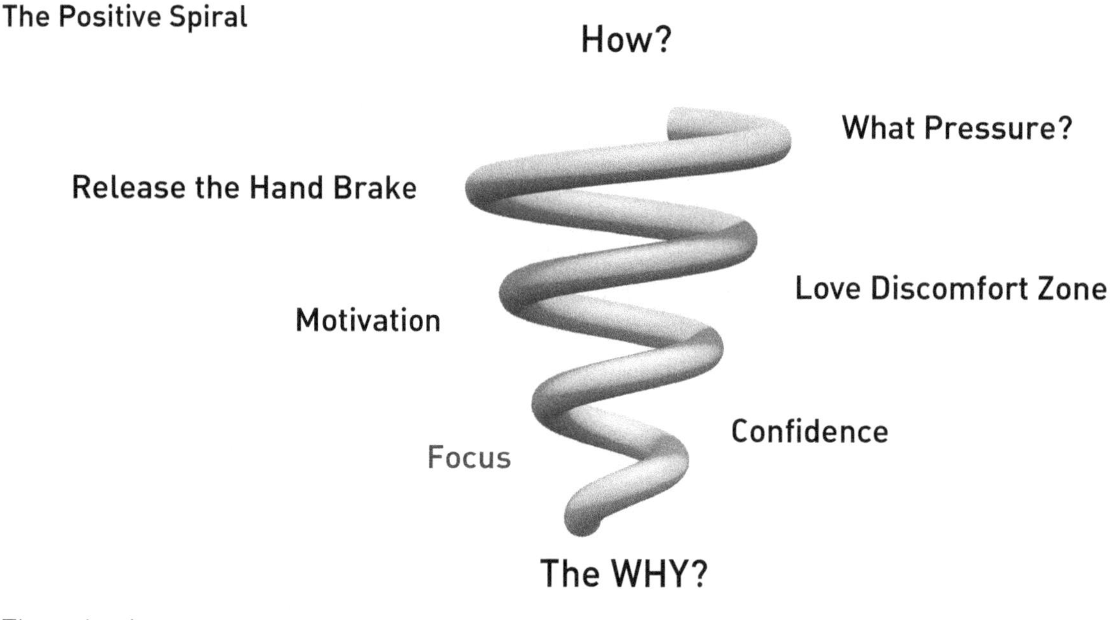

There is also a *negative spiral*.

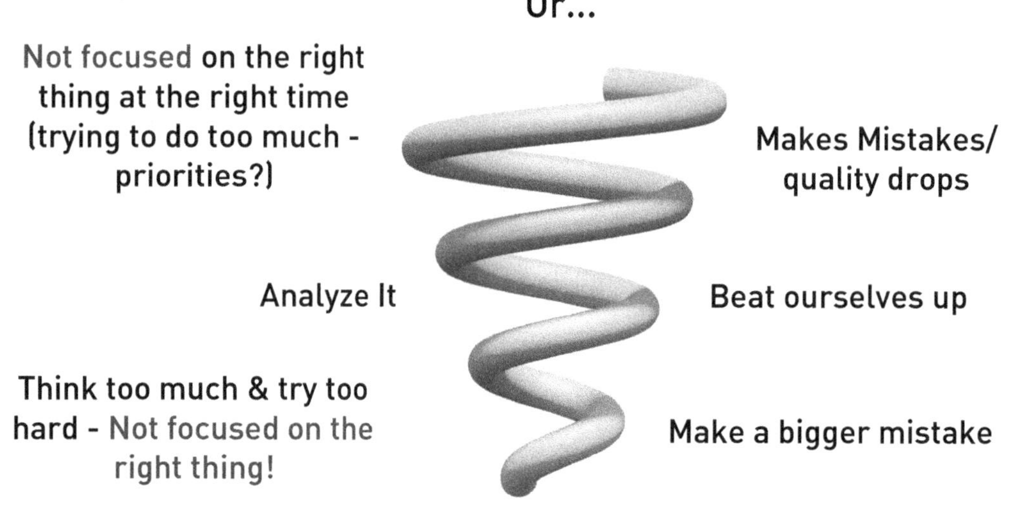

When we're not focused on the right thing at the right time, we often end up making a mistake. When that happens, most people want to know why it went wrong. So, they start to analyze their performance. They also beat themselves up. Then they start to over-think their performance, try too hard and force things. As a result, they go and make a bigger mistake. If this keeps going, their performance crashes.

I suspect that you'll have noticed the vital element here, which dictates whether we rise through the positive spiral or slide down the negative spiral.

That's right... it's FOCUS.

How to Hone Focus

I have found that the best starting point is to simplify the job. Cut out the complexity and start with a straightforward task that is entirely under the control of the performer[12]. In a team environment, this means that everyone needs to have a simple job. They have to know what they need to do and how to do it. As a coach or manager, that is arguably one of our most important jobs[13].

Do you remember Chris Cook, the swimmer we discussed earlier? To give you a little background, Chris and I worked together for around seven years. We met up in 2001. He'd just returned from the World Student Games and had come home disappointed with his performance. He had become really anxious before the competitions; he didn't sleep, couldn't eat and was so nervous he would be sick. At that time, he wasn't a star swimmer by any means. He was an average regional level athlete and wasn't on Team GB's radar.

Chris retired from competitive swimming in 2008. His is last competitive race was an Olympic Final in Beijing. As he hung up his swimming cap and goggles, Chris was a double Olympian, an Olympic finalist, double Commonwealth Champion, double Commonwealth record holder and seventh fastest swimmer in the history of his event.

So, what happened between 2001 and 2008?

Importantly there was one moment early in 2004, which Chris describes as a "career defining moment", when we actually understood Chris' job. At that point, we realized that Chris' job was simply to swim two lengths of the pool as fast as he could, and that was it, nothing else!

Until that moment, we'd been confused.
We thought that his job was to win.
It wasn't!
We thought his job was to make the British team.
It wasn't!
Or, to secure sponsorship or funding.
It wasn't that either!

Chris' job was a 100m swimmer in a 50m pool. His job was just to swim two lengths of the pool as fast as he could.

When he just focused on doing that, he became brilliant. That simple task became his single point of focus, every day, for the next four years. Everything he did, in every training session, every day, contributed to swimming two lengths of the pool as fast as possible. His job, in every competition, no matter how big or small, was simply to swim two lengths of the pool as fast as he could.
And that was it!

Importantly, I also asked Chris to tell me the five key things he needed to do in order to swim two lengths as fast as he could. These were the five most important things. They were the five that had the greatest impact on his performance.

Once we'd identified his top five, we focused all of our energies on improving these. And, on competition day, he would focus on executing these five key processes as well as he could.

Chris' Five Keys were...

1. Start Fast.
2. Fast, but efficient, first length.
3. Quick turn.
4. Hold my speed for as long as I can on the second length.
5. Touch the wall with two hands. (if you don't do that in breaststroke you are disqualified)

So, what are your "Two Lengths of the Pool"?
What's your job in the simplest possible terms?

This is not a goal or a target! It is a process, not an outcome. Therefore, it is completely under your control. It is also a complete statement of success.

Once you know your Two Lengths of the Pool, see if you can identify your Five Keys.

Which are the five most important processes in your performance? Which five have the greatest impact on your performance? If you could only pick five, which ones would you choose?

Once you know these, you have a really powerful way of honing your focus and helping your players do the same. Rather than worrying about winning and losing, what would happen if you simply focused on scoring as many goals as possible and conceding as few as possible? What would happen if every player did this from kick off to the final whistle? Imagine if everyone dedicated themselves to this during each and every practice.

How good could you become?

If you want to hone your focus, start by...

*   Simplifying and clarifying your job.
*   Identifying the key processes.
*   Focus on executing these as well as you possibly can.

How to Control Confidence

I don't talk about building confidence or increasing confidence. I talk about controlling confidence. Is your confidence under your control?

Crucially, confidence is built on evidence, not pep talks or affirmation cards. In the performance spiral, when we focus on the right thing at the right time, we begin performing well. This gives us evidence that we can do it. It's that evidence that fuels our confidence.

So, if confidence is built on evidence, there are a couple of questions.
What evidence are you using to underpin your confidence?
How can you build a strong bank of evidence, that can power your confidence?

Let's take question one first.
What evidence are you using to underpin your confidence?

Here is a selection of possible sources that we could use. Some of these are under our control. Some are not. Which ones do we have control over, and which are outside of our control?

- Cheers and boos from the crowd?
- The result.
- Feedback from coaches.
- Feedback from parents.
- Our own honest, objective evaluation of our performance.
- Comments on social media.
- Selection or de-selection from the team.
- Feedback from team-mates.
- Our game stats.

I would argue that only one of these is genuinely under our control. Can you identify which one it is?
That's right – Our own honest, objective evaluation of our performance.

The others lie outside of our control. For example, we can't control whether the crowd cheer us or boo us (although what we do might influence that). Equally, we don't control the result. The opposition and referee tend to have a significant impact on the score. We don't control other people's feedback (whether it comes from coaches, parents, other players or via social media). Other people always decide what they say.

If we draw our confidence from these sources, we hand over the remote control for our confidence to someone else or something else. Therefore, our confidence is not under our control.

To bring confidence back under our control, we need to honestly and objectively evaluate our performance. This is very different from judging ourselves on our results, or on other people's feedback.

If we honestly and objectively evaluate our performance, we can start to answer question two as well.

Our second question is…
How can you build a strong bank of evidence, that can power your confidence?

When we evaluate our performance honestly and objectively, we identify those things we did well and those things we want to improve.

For example, let's say you scored your performance 6/10. There will be things you did well, which made your score 6/10 not 0/10. However, it can't have been perfect because it wasn't 10/10. So, there are things you will want to improve. If you identify things you're going to work on, and commit to improving them, you'll come back better. This is a very simple, but incredibly powerful, way of growing your confidence.

To be honest, it doesn't matter whether you score 2/10 or 8/10, as long as you don't start to judge yourself. If you score 2/10, simply identify what you did well and what you're working on. Then work on it and know that when you play next, you'll be better than a 2/10. Then go again. Each game you'll keep getting better.

When we adopt this approach, our confidence comes from the evidence that we are improving. When I work with elite level athletes (including the world champions and professional players), their confidence often comes from the quality of their preparation. I'll often ask them how confident they are feeling before an event. They normally answer by telling me how well they've practiced, trained and prepared. If they have been highly focused, practiced with real quality, pushed themselves in training and seen improvement, they will feel confident. If they ducked out of some training or if they know they haven't given their all, they are far less likely to feel confident.

So, if we want to bring confidence back into our control...

- Evaluate your performance, honestly and objectively.
- Work on the areas you want to improve.
- Know that you've done everything possible in your practice, training and preparation.

How to Master Motivation

Motivation is often known as "the why of behavior". In sport, understanding our "why" is critical. Why are we there? Why do we play soccer or coach soccer? What's our reason?
Our "why" is critically important because it guides our focus.

Very simply...
Focus follows interest
And
Interest follows what we really care about.

If we want to perform well, we need to focus on the process. When we focus on the process, we tend to execute well, and our performance follows.

However, it's really tough to focus on the process if we care too much about the outcome. If we focus on the outcome, we are not focused on the process. As a result, we tend to over-think, try too hard, force things and make mistakes.

I one had a conversation with an elite tennis player. He was really struggling with his game. During our conversation, I asked him why he played tennis. He told me it was all about winning.

In professional tennis, winning is important. Winning equals prize money. If he doesn't win, he won't get paid. However, when we delved a little deeper, he talked about the social importance of winning. He talked about what everyone would think of him if he wasn't winning. He described winning, and his ranking, like some kind of social currency. It gave him a feeling of status and respect from his community. These were the real reasons he played tennis and needed to win.

Then, I said something that sounded ridiculous to him. I said, "You need to be more interested and care more about how you hit the ball, than where it lands". Immediately, he started to argue that it didn't matter how he hit it, as long as it landed the right side of the white line. However, as we talked about it a little more, he realized that if he was too focused on where it landed, he wasn't focused on how he hit it.

And, the only way to play decent shots is to focus on how you hit the ball. His challenge, of course, was to care more about the process than he did about the result.

Why?
Because focus follows interest… and interest follows what you really care about.
So, what's your "why"?
Why do you coach?
Is it for the players?
Is it to be the best coach?
Is it to win trophies or championships as a coach?
Is it to gain respect from others?

What about your players?
What is their "why"?
Do they just love playing?
Do they want to be the best they can be?
Do they have ambitions to get a college scholarship, turn pro or play internationally?
Are they trying to impress their parents, or make them proud?

Our "why" is also critical for another important reason. If our reason for playing (or coaching) starts to disappear, our motivation tends to go with it. For example, if our "why" revolves around winning and we start losing back-to-back games, our motivation could start to dry up. When we lose our reason to do something, we start to ask, "What's the point?".
What's the point in working my butt off in training if I'm not winning?
What's the point in putting in all the effort and all the hours if noone notices?
Why am I bothering if I'm not getting selected?

Motivation is an absolutely vital element of mental toughness.
It powers our tenacity, our ability to keep going when every fibre of our being is begging us to stop.
It underpins our resilience, our ability to get up whenever we get knocked down.

It impacts on our ability to be composed: to focus on the right thing at the right time, which allows us to make great decisions and execute well when it really matters.

So, what is your "why"?

Practical Guide

So, here's a little practical guide to summarize those key points.

Focus

Simplify and clarify your job.
Understand your job "Two Lengths of the Pool".
Focus on delivering your "Two Lengths".
Understand your key processes and effective points of focus.
Focus on the processes!

Confidence

Practice and prepare as well as you possibly can.
Know that you have a great game plan.
Know you can execute it.
After your performance... evaluate your performance, honestly and objectively.
Don't judge yourself on the results!

Motivation

Have a solid "why".
Remember... Focus follows interest and interest follows what you really care about.

Coaching Masterclass

Here is an example from an equestrian rider that I worked with a few years ago:

"It's 2 weeks until the competition, which is obviously your big focus at the moment. It's probably fair to say that it is not just a big focus because it's in 2 weeks' time. This competition also represents your big ambition in the sport at this point and has been a focus for years.

We discussed how you're feeling about it right now. Your words were 'scared, nervous and worried'. You also talked about the 'pressure of competing for this team in this competition'. We spent quite a while chatting about where this stems from. You talked about missing the opportunity a couple of years ago and not being ready last year. You also talked about the time and money invested into training and competition. You mentioned the pressure that you have perceived when competing for this team, because it is high profile and there are people watching, etc.

They are all common reasons why people feel nervous before events. In reality, what people do is they tend to attach a lot of meaning to an event, which acts as baggage and forms an agenda that is not really there."

As we continued to talk, it became obvious that there were other issues at play as well:

"You mentioned that typically you have not been confident in yourself. This has also manifested in your work and life. If we are not confident in life, we tend to pin all of our self-worth on the results we get from sport. In a sense, we look to our sporting success or failure to tell us how good we are at life. In this situation, we rely on good results for our self-acceptance and therefore place massive pressure on the performance. As I said, I believe that there is no such thing as pressure. It is created by our imagination. It has to be imaginary because it is a future event. The only place it can exist is our imagination. The fact is that because we create it, we can also get rid of it! Ultimately, you will feel less pressure to perform in competition when you start to see it for what it really is. The job is actually pretty simple when you look at it – you just need to jump over as many fences as you can as quickly as you can. If it starts to become more than that, we get into problems.

The reality is that the job doesn't change just because it's a major competition. It wouldn't change if we put it into an arena with 100 TV cameras and called it an Olympic final, or if it was a training session in your own paddock. We talked about how you can build your confidence and become happy competing. As you said, priority number 1 is to have fun and enjoy it because that's the whole point in riding!! We also talked about how your performance is dependent upon your focus. If you are thinking 'I hope I don't hit the fence', then you're more likely to hit it. If said to you, 'don't think about the color blue', then your mind will be filled with blue. The only way to turn this around is to start focusing on the things that will help you perform. As we chatted about it, you said that you ride at your best when you're focused on the sound of the horses' hooves. If you can really immerse yourself in that sort of focus, your performance will start to take care of itself.

You also know that you can perform well. You have performed well recently (within the last couple of weeks) and cleared fences that you probably wouldn't have imagined you could clear. Your confidence is built upon evidence. Evidence tells you that you can clear the fences because you do it in training. If you can make training as challenging as competition, you will find it easier to see competition in the same way that you see training. Train like you compete and compete like you train!"

In order to start turning their performance around, most people need a very simple starting point. They may see their task as bewildering, maybe even impossible. This is normally a result of getting the job wrong in the first place. We will explore this in much greater detail later.

Simply understanding that our clarity of focus often underpins our confidence is the starting point and understanding that our confidence often underpins our motivation is the next stage.

Here is another example from a session I did with a martial artist, who was frustrated by his recent slump in form:

"In order to help you to break the pattern that you are in, I asked you about the mental baggage that you are carrying at the moment. We started this by talking about why it is important to win. You said that winning was important because it tells you that you've done what you are capable of. This is important because you know that your training is coming together and you are heading in the right direction. I asked what the right direction is. You said 'becoming the British Champion'. I also asked why it's important to become the British Champion. You said that it proves to yourself and everyone else that you can do it. We started to talk about 'everyone else'. You started to tell me about your mates and the blokes at the gym. You also said that until you were 22 you were bullied and that being a martial arts champion would help you to counter that.

The problem is that it creates false pressure. It acts like a sack of bricks on your back, weighing you down. It clutters your mind and creates too much mental noise. It stops you from doing the very, very simple job of fighting the best fight you can. Fighting the best fight you can, on the day, is your ONLY job. The job is not to win. It is not to qualify for anything. It is not to impress anyone or make anyone else happy or proud. Stick to a very simple, clear focus. We chatted briefly about the best point of focus for you. I asked you 'what is the single most important thing you need to focus on when you are fighting?'. You said, 'watch the opponent's eyes'. Keep it simple, watch the opponent's eyes and let your instinct and skills do the rest."

These principles don't just apply to sports. They apply equally to any other walk of life. Here is an example from the first session of an Executive Coaching program with the leader of a high-profile business, who was frustrated because he was working a huge number of hours but struggling to move the business forward at the pace he desired:

"You mentioned that although you know you should focus your attention, you are easily distracted.

I asked the question, 'if you had a magic wand, how would things look?'. You started by saying that there really aren't enough hours in the day. You need to start focusing on your workload and being effective with your time. As we discussed this, you mentioned in passing that you are a 'bit of a control freak'. In the same breath, you also said that all of your directors are better than you in their respective fields. You trust them and are happy to let them run with projects. However, you also get yourself sucked into meetings that you may not need to be in.

In our ideal picture we see you with more strategic thinking time and strategic execution time. You are less involved in proofreading, answering questions that aren't yours, less tied up in the minutiae and meetings that don't involve you.

We also discussed a future where you work closely with your directors to drive corporate objectives. You mentioned spending more time on your visible external profile, winning new clients and exploring market opportunities. It would also allow you to take a more strategic look at the internal structure and culture within the business.

Step 1 is to clarify and simplify your role to ensure that you can be as effective as possible. We need to sharpen your focus so that you know exactly where you should direct your energies to have the maximum possible impact. Once we do that, you stand a very good chance of both reducing the number of hours at your desk and making more of an impact on the business. It all starts by understanding where you need to be focused. What are the most effective things?"

Some Vital Resources

To help you understand how to engineer your headspace, here are some videos that Simon put together…

What's On Your iPad? - **https://youtu.be/Tg4yMTZqa9c**

To find out more about Performance Spirals
Performance Spirals - **https://youtu.be/r7lO9XNv2SE**

To help you Hone Focus…
Hone Focus - **https://youtu.be/-c8QZl5UlyU**
Two Lengths of the Pool - **https://youtu.be/aXr8rzW2q88**
And **https://www.amazon.com/Two-Lengths-Pool-Sometimes-simplest/dp/1484969855/**

To learn how to Control Confidence…
Control Confidence - **https://youtu.be/R00AbvVfFcl**

To learn more about how to Master Motivation…
Master Motivation - **https://youtu.be/DJTohmyIFE8**

Key Points to Take Home

- Focus, confidence and motivation are all fundamental to peak performance.
- Focus, confidence and motivation are all interdependent. They require each other.
- Focus underpins confidence.
- Confidence underpins motivation.
- To turn around a performance, it

Summarizing Stage Two

Congratulations. You've taken another huge stride on your way to becoming a Mental Toughness Master!

Now that you've completed Stage Two, you will understand the following:

1. How to consistently engineer a solid mental game in your players:
   - ✓ Ensure that your team is consistently focused, confident and motivated
   - ✓ Understand that motivation, confidence and focus are all dependent upon each other
2. How to help your players to hone their focus:
   - ✓ Simplify and clarify the task
   - ✓ Focus on the processes
   - ✓ Focus through the senses
3. How to coach players to control their confidence:
   - ✓ Evaluate the performance, honestly and objectively
   - ✓ Build on what you can do
4. How to assist your players to master their motivation:
   - ✓ Know the reason
5. How to coach your players to de-construct 'pressure':
   - ✓ Pressure is imaginary
   - ✓ Get the job right

The Next Step...

Stage 3 – Accountability & Responsibility

Once players are able to hone their focus, control confidence and master motivation, we can start to develop accountability and responsibility. In doing so, we will cultivate their ability to absorb, use and ultimately to seek out critical feedback to improve. We will also explore the way world class performers approach uncertainty, failures, challenges and set-backs, and how we can foster these qualities in players.

During Stage 3, you will learn how to coach your players to become accountable and responsible for their performance. With these skills, players will gain far greater control over their performance and their development.

Are you ready to get cracking?

STAGE THREE: ACCOUNTABILITY AND RESPONSIBILITY

We want to be able to explore the following issues in this section:

- Harnessing focus
- Controlled confidence
- Master motivation
- Acknowledging and Using critical feedback for improvement
- Dealing with uncertainty
- Handling failure
- Managing challenges and setbacks
- 5 Keys of accountability
- Taking responsibility and control
- Standards and expectations
- Summary of interview with Chris Cook

Welcome to Stage Three – Accountability & Responsibility

Welcome to Stage Three. By this point you will know what Mental Toughness is, what it looks like and how to recognize it. You have some ways of assessing Mental Toughness (such as The Mental Toughness Matrix). During Stage Two, you will have learned some practical strategies to consistently engineer an optimal mind-set. This will help you to achieve your best performances consistently.

Stage 1 – Understanding Mental Toughness (Complete)
Stage 2 – Consistent Optimal Performance (You are here)
Stage 3 – Accountability and Responsibility (You ate here)
Stage 4 – Enter The Discomfort Zone
Stage 5 – Toughness; Tenacity, Resilience and Composure

Great Foundations

Right at the start of this book (Understanding Mental Toughness), we said that each stage provided a foundation for the next. It is a bit like building a staircase; you cannot build the second step, until you have the first.

In reality, it is very difficult to develop accountability, unless you have a clear focus. A few years ago I worked with an English Championship football club. They were struggling. In fact, they were heading for relegation. After one match, I listened in as their manager was talking to the players. The manager was annoyed because the team had lost and everyone had performed below par.

In a heated discussion, the manager turned to the players and said:

"Why will nobody take accountability?"

When I chatted to the manager later, I asked him to explain each player's job. I asked the following:

"What are the five key things that each player is expected to do?"

Unfortunately, the manager and his coaching staff were vague. They did not know exactly what they expected from each of the players. Consequently, they had not told the players what was expected with any clarity. If we have a simple, clear task, we can be held accountable for delivering it. It needs to be clearly defined. We need to know what to deliver. Once we agreed upon the five key things with each player, we could then hold them accountable for delivering them.

It's also vital that we identify processes, not outcomes. I asked the manager what each player was expected to do. By asking this question, I am asking about processes. For example, you can't hold a team accountable for winning, because it's not entirely under the team's control. Equally, you can't hold a center forward accountable for scoring, because that too is an outcome. There are a huge number of elements that are outside of the center forward's control, such as the quality of the assists they receive and the performance of the opposing goalkeeper. However, you can hold them accountable for the processes.

Why Is This Stage So Important?

Those who blame other people and misfortune will not become mentally tough. Mentally tough athletes take complete responsibility for their performance.

In fact, it goes further than that. In my studies of world class performers, I discovered that it is a characteristic they all share. In fact, taking responsibility is one of the eight key characteristics that differentiate world class performers. In How to Shine[1], Olympic Finalist and Double Gold Medalist, Chris Cook, describes how responsibility and control are inseparable. Multiple Michelin Star Chef, Kenny Atkinson, also explains how he builds Mental Toughness and world-class standards in his team through accountability and responsibility.

This is a vital stage in the process and a key ingredient of Mental Toughness.

During this stage, you will learn:

1. Why we need to take responsibility if we wish to take control
2. How world-class performers and athletes develop accountability & responsibility in themselves and their teams
3. Why focus is crucial in developing accountability and responsibility
4. How to coach a successful mind-set within your players

Let's go!

Responsibility and Mental Toughness

How Do World Class Performers Develop Mental Toughness?

Let's take some expert advice from…
Kenny Atkinson: Multiple Michelin Starred Chef
Chris Cook: Double Olympian
Alan Hinkes: World-Leading Mountaineer
Alison Waters: World Number 3 Squash Player
Chris Robertson: England Squash's National Head Coach and Head of Performance, Keir Worth.
Bruce Duncan: World-Leading Adventure Racer
Andy McMenemy: World-Record Breaking Ultra Distance Runner
Ben Saunders: Record-Breaking Polar Explorer

How Is Mental Toughness Developed?

There is very strong evidence telling us that mental toughness is crucial for those who want to be the best they can be. But, how is mental toughness created? How is it developed?

Is mental toughness something which is innate, or can it be nurtured through experience? In an autobiographical account of his experiences as a prisoner in Nazi concentration camps, Viktor Frankl14 noticed that the 'toughest' men were not the most physically robust, but the ones with inner fortitude. He explains that those with deep spiritual and moral foundations were the ones who could bear more suffering. Certainly, these traits are unlikely to be innate.

Knowing the importance of mental toughness, Michelin starred chef, Kenny Atkinson, works to develop it in his team. He explains the process that he uses in the kitchen:

"Toughness and resilience comes through maintaining the standards, giving responsibility and making people accountable. I am really pushing the guys here to get the Michelin star. It's not easy. I learned it the same way. Chefs pushed me, made me responsible for upholding standards in my section and held me accountable. You cannot have any excuses, you have to make sure you're on the ball constantly, even though you do not feel up to it some days".

The process that Kenny uses in the kitchen is based on some fundamental principles, such as discipline. Alan Hinkes, explains how this applies to mountaineering:

"I think you can develop toughness, yes. In the military, it's called discipline, training and drill. Now I think there is a difference between being mentally tough and doing things automatically. To develop toughness, you uphold standards and push people to take on tougher challenges".

These base principles also appear to be central in developing the next group of world-class squash players. Chris Robertson and Keir Worth explain.

Chris says:

"I think toughness can be trained, absolutely. Being on time is important, keeping diaries is important, exhibiting a professional attitude, responsibility, attention to detail, how they prepare and do things when they are here. We're looking to see how prepared they are when they play. We are looking for situations where they are challenged. Today we have situations where lower ranked players are playing higher ranked players. The first thing I'm looking for is whether they approach the game the same way as they normally would. Are they going to take everything they can from the match? When things start going against them, which will probably happen, are they going to pack up and go home or are they going to dig in and decide this is the time and it's my last chance to stay in this match? As coaches, we have these off-the-cuff situations. Formalizing that takes a lot of doing. We will use a lot of video analysis; go back, make notes, assess behavior, assess reaction to different situations, etc.

"I think toughness can be trained, absolutely. Being on time is important, keeping diaries is important, exhibiting a professional attitude, responsibility, attention to detail, how they prepare and do things when they are here. We're looking to see how prepared they are when they play. We are looking for situations where they are challenged. Today we have situations where lower ranked players are playing higher ranked players. The first thing I'm looking for is whether they approach the game the same way as they normally would. Are they going to take everything they can from the match? When things start going against them, which will probably happen, are they going to pack up and go home or are they going to dig in and decide this is the time and it's my last chance to stay in this match? As coaches, we have these off-the-cuff situations. Formalizing that takes a lot of doing. We will use a lot of video analysis; go back, make notes, assess behavior, assess reaction to different situations, etc.

That's why the upbringing and how they are at home and with their parents has such an impact, because it conditions how you are to be. For me as a sports coach, you're looking to develop those behaviors all the time. And we can start to build that picture up. We spend time talking to players at those critical moments.

Today players will be put in situations where they have to stand up if they want to be a top player. They will be in tough situations and they will have to respond. And if they fail, that's okay, but they learn how to be more tough and that there are parts of the game you have to be tough. They can start to recognize that this is the time I need to give my best and not shirk away. Because if you want to be a great player, you have to answer that challenge."

Keir says:

"Traditionally, we have hoped that it will emerge through the competitive framework. The challenge of tough competition helps to develop a tough mentality. Now though, I think we have to do more than that. I think it emerges with good coaches and what good coaches do on a daily basis with players. Coaches create boundaries, they talk to players about what it acceptable and what is not, behavior on court and off court, developing players as professionals. It develops through the coach player relationship, which requires a significant amount of coach development. It is crucially important. You cannot get away from the role parents play and their boundaries as to what is acceptable. We do use senior players to help share their experiences to those lower down."

Interestingly, there are common themes that run though all of these accounts: discipline, professionalism, accountability and continual challenge.

Mental toughness is underpinned by traits such as discipline, accountability and professionalism. They are central to success, and go hand in hand with responsibility. Viktor Frankl[14] points out that the word responsible ('response-able') means that we are 'able to respond'.

Ultimately, these world class performers know that the responsibility for their success, and in some cases their survival, stops with them.

World number three squash player, Alison Waters:

"Professional squash players are self-employed, so you have to take responsibility for your own performance. When I was younger, I used to rely on other people more. I used to spend a lot of time with my coach. I'd turn up for a session and he'd tell me what the session was. That was kinda fine at the time because I was younger and probably needed that help. I guess I did not think too much, I just turned up and trained. Now-a-days I will do my own thing much more. I still have people around me, like my strength and conditioning coach, my physiotherapist and the technical coaches. But I think you get to the stage where there is only so much you can get from others. It's down to me at the end of the day. If I turn up for a coaching lesson now, I will suggest to the coach that we work on this or that. It's changed around now. The coaches won't dictate what we work on: they will ask. It means that I do not turn up for a session for the sake of it; I really need to get something from it. The physiotherapist could give me endless amounts of programs, but if I do not do them, I will not benefit."

Alison knows that taking responsibility has a tangible importance. In reality, her success on court has a direct impact on her livelihood. Mountaineer Alan Hinkes knows that those who fail to take responsibility may pay the ultimate price.

"With the very best mountaineers and guides, taking responsibility just comes as second nature. I've always accepted that I am responsible for what I do. A lot of people might think, 'oh well there's a rescue team'. But they cannot always get to you, especially on the big mountains. In Britain you could maybe get away with it, but right from the start I've never wanted anyone to have to rescue me. We've always had the mind that we want to get ourselves off the hill. I guess we were more self-sufficient a few years ago. It was more difficult to get a rescue team in them days.

We'd have to get to the nearest farm, or telephone box to get help and by the time you've done that, you may as well have got yourself off the hill. These days I think people are probably less self-sufficient because they can always get on the cell phone. In the Himalaya, there are not any rescue teams, so you have to be self-sufficient. There are not any helicopters. You can't get a helicopter over 6000 meters realistically.

You're on your own on the 8000-meter peaks and that's why I pushed myself to do them, because you're not artificially on your own, you're really on your own. In the UK, you could say that you'll not use your cell phone, but that's a bit artificial. Go to an 8000'er and it's for real."

Relationship to Performance

Australian sport psychologist, Phil Jauncey[15], considers that responsibility and accountability are central to performance. He has worked with many of Australia's leading sports teams, notably in cricket and rugby league. In his book, Managing Yourself & Others, Phil Jauncey argues that many people suffer from a modern day cultural disease; they believe that it's okay to fail, as long as they feel good about it. Rather than looking for ways to address the issues that are causing them to fail, they look instead for excuses. To sum up his point, he says, 'I believe very strongly that everything I do is my responsibility and, therefore, if I do not like what I am doing I can change it'. So, as Phil Jauncey suggests, responsibility goes hand-in-hand with control and choice.

Record breaking ultra-distance athlete Andy McMenemy agrees:

"No-one else can do this. It's me. I've got to get through this. I chose to do this. No one is making me. It is part of the territory. This is what it takes. If it was easy, everyone would be doing it. I heard a saying that you 'grow through' tough times, not 'go through' them. If I can get passed this, I can do anything. If it was easy, everyone would be doing it."

These sentiments are shared by a number of our other world class interviewees. Polar explorer, Ben Saunders continues:

"In 2003, I did a shorter solo expedition. A solo trip seemed like the ultimate level of challenge. If I was on my own I could not rely on anyone else. It was a two-week expedition. Everything went right. I had more control because it was down to me."

Double Olympian, Chris Cook was even more direct in his assessment:

"We need to cut out that word 'blame'. It really should not come in."

The message is clear! World-class performers do not blame or make excuses. They take full responsibility for their performance. They also know that responsibility, accountability, professionalism and discipline are absolutely fundamental in developing Mental Toughness!

Coaches Workshop on Taking Responsibility

These world-class performers have shared some critical insights as to how they develop accountability and responsibility in themselves and their teams.

Here are a few of their key take-away messages.

Multiple Michelin Star Chef, Kenny Atkinson

KEY MESSAGE:
"You cannot enforce a standard if your team does not know what the standard is."

- We learn from mistakes when we take responsibility for them, and accept them.
- Take criticism on board and use it to make you stronger.
- Kenny does not allow his chefs to get comfortable.
- Develop trust in your team by working with them and training them

Gold Medal Winning Swimmer, Chris Cook
KEY MESSAGE:
"When you take responsibility, something magical happens... you start to take control."

- Champions have a certain work ethic – they are the first ones at training, helping to set up for the session.
- You have to learn from the tough challenges. Sometimes the toughest challenges give the greatest lessons.
- You only learn when you take responsibility for the performance.
- Ego can get in the way if you let it.
- Failures are actually just a bunch of opportunities.
- Take responsibility for every session, so that you get the most from every moment.

Thing about ten things in your own practice and experience to answer the following question:

How can you learn from these accounts to develop accountability and responsibility in your team?

Trapdoor for Coaches

When you listen to coaches being interviewed in the media, how often do you hear these words:

"It was the referee's fault"

"We were just unlucky"

"We need to credit to the opposition, they were the better team today"

"When you're struggling for a result, you just don't seem to get those breaks"

"If we can just get a lucky break, we'll be okay"

All of these messages say one thing:

"It's not my fault"

What message does that send out to the rest of the team?

- Excuses are okay here.
- Blame other people and circumstances if things go wrong.
- We need luck (because we cannot perform well without it)

If the coach makes excuses and fails to take responsibility, how do you think the players will respond?

As a coach, what can you do to lead by example?

What are the Key Messages that you picked up from reading about Responsibility and Mental Toughness?

How can you incorporate those into your coaching and the culture of your team?

Summarizing Stage Three

Congratulations. You've taken another huge stride on your way to becoming a Mental Toughness Master!

Now that you've completed Stage Three, you will understand...

1. Why we need to take responsibility if we wish to take control:

✓ It is a message that is reinforced by Olympic finalist Chris Cook and other world-class performers.

2. How world-class performers and athletes develop accountability & responsibility in themselves and their teams:

✓ By making people accountable for upholding standards

3. Why focus is crucial in developing accountability and responsibility:

✓ We need a simple, clear focus.

✓ We need to know the standard.

✓ Once we have those, we can uphold the standard.

4. How to coach a successful mind-set within your players:

✓ Discipline and professionalism are central.

✓ That does not come by shouting at players or by drilling them. It comes when we understand the importance of those tiny details.

The Next Step…

Stage 4 – Enter "The Discomfort Zone"

Once players have started to be accountable and accept responsibility, we can really optimize their 'discomfort zone.' We will look at ways in which world class performers become mentally tough by using their discomfort zone to push their own boundaries. In doing so, we will study the methods that world leading organizations and world class individuals use to develop toughness.

Let's really start to ramp this up now!

STAGE FOUR: ENTERING 'THE DISCOMFORT ZONE'

We will be focusing on the following things in this stage:

1.   Building mental toughness
2.   Pushing boundaries
3.   Constructing and maintaining resilience
4.   Identification of critical standards
5.   Finding and Loving your discomfort zone
6.   Staying ahead

Welcome to Stage Four – Enter 'The Discomfort Zone'

Welcome to Stage Four. By this point you will know what Mental Toughness is, what it looks like and how to recognize it. You'll have some ways of assessing Mental Toughness (using The Mental Toughness Matrix). During Stage Two, you will have learned some practical strategies to consistently engineer an optimal mind-set. This will help you to achieve your best performances consistently. Stage Three will have taught you how to develop accountability and responsibility in your players.

Stage 1 – Understand Mental Toughness (Complete)

Stage 2 – Consistent Optimal Performance (Complete)

Stage 3 – Accountability and Responsibility (Complete)

Stage 4 – Enter The Discomfort Zone (You are here)

Stage 5 – Toughness; Tenacity, Resilience and Composure

Your Foundation

Entering our Discomfort Zone is often tough. Typically, most people will seek comfort, rather than discomfort. People tend to operate within their comfort zone, rather than push themselves into their Discomfort Zone. Interestingly, world class performers continually push themselves into discomfort.

When we refer to The Discomfort Zone, we are not just referring to physical comfort. Our Discomfort Zone can extend to many different facets of our life. Some people are uncomfortable when asked to relinquish control. Others become uncomfortable when they receive critical feedback, or when they are challenges to deliver higher standards. When we become aware of the breadth of our Comfort and Discomfort Zones, we can start to see the need to build a solid foundation.

Those people who venture into their Discomfort Zones tend to have self-belief and are motivated. During Stage Two, we identified strategies to build confidence, motivation and focus. In addition, people who are happy to step outside of their comfort zone are also those who are willing to take responsibility for their performance and learn from their mistakes.

As we have already learned, Mental Toughness is underpinned by accountability and responsibility. If these foundation blocks are missing, it will be tough for people to take significant strides outside of their Comfort Zone and explore their Discomfort Zone.

Why Is This Stage So Important?

Mental Toughness is developed when people push their own limits. As we push our boundaries, we extend the scope of what we can do. By challenging ourselves to do things we are not comfortable with, we become tougher. Throughout this Stage Four of Master Mental Toughness, you will see how world-class performers have pushed through their limits and become capable of extraordinary feats. The strategies they use are available to us all.

During this stage, you will learn:

1. How the world's greatest sports organizations and individuals stay ahead by continually pushing themselves into their Discomfort Zone.
2. The importance of pushing, making mistakes and using them to get better!
3. How world class performers approach uncertainty, set-backs and challenges.
4. How to identify your Discomfort Zone and use it to improve your performance.
5. How to use an understanding of 'critical standards' to improve performance.

Let's go!

Learn from Everything

You need to take the first steps into your discomfort zone. Here are some insights from a genuine sporting legend, Michael Jordan:

"I've missed more than 9000 shots in my career. I've lost almost 300 games. 26 times, I've been trusted to take the game winning shot and missed. I've failed over and over and over again in my life. And that is why I succeed."

Michael Jordan is not alone. Most of the great people who have ever lived, have failed. Many of the great entrepreneurs went bust numerous times before they made serious money. The great artists and composers have torn up more work than they ever published. Great athletes always miss more than they score and make more duff shots than perfect shots. And, as Michael Jordan says, that is the reason they succeed[16].

Those people that venture into their Discomfort Zones tend to have self-belief and are motivated. During Stage Two, we identified strategies to build confidence, motivation and focus. In addition, people who are happy to step outside of their comfort zone are also those who are willing to take responsibility for their performance and learn from their mistakes.

It is funny how most people hate making mistakes. As human beings, we tend to view mistakes as negative. We tend to view bad performances and losing as negative. In reality though, it's not the case. I agree that it's usually uncomfortable at the time. Most of us would prefer everything to work perfectly all the time. We want things to come off perfectly the first time and often get frustrated if the results don't show quickly enough.

Everyone knows that making mistakes is an important part of the learning process. However, there are relatively few people that embrace mistakes and celebrate them, or who even see them as a positive. Common advice is to forget about bad performances and put them behind you. However, the impact of losing or performing badly does often drive people to work harder on their game. However, research shows that most people learn the least about their performance from victories or successes[17].

One of the characteristics of a truly great athlete is that they learn from everything – the good, the bad and the average. They learn from wonderful performances and dire performances equally. Those truly great athletes realize that to stay ahead, they don't just need to move forwards. They need to move forwards quicker than everyone else, or they'll get overtaken. At the very pinnacle of every sport are athletes who constantly improve their game. They have to get better after every single training session and every single match they play. If they don't, they know that someone will overtake them.

How quickly are you moving forwards? Are you better than you were at this point last season? Are you better than you were last month? Are you better than you were last week? Are you better today than you were yesterday? It is probably quite easy to say that you're better than a year ago. But what about a week ago? Have you improved in the last week? Have you used each moment and every opportunity to improve? There are countless learning opportunities available. They are available to everyone. Some people recognize them and get the benefit of them. Other people miss them.

Reflection is the key!

It doesn't have to be a heavy exercise. Taking time out while driving home from a game or a training session is often a really good way of examining the learning opportunities. It can be as simple as asking yourself, "What did I do well?", "What do I need to work on?", "How might I do it differently next time?"[16]

In reality, many athletes don't tend to review their performances on a regular basis or in any real depth. They don't really step back and look at how their game is progressing. For professional athletes, the off-season usually provides a good opportunity for reviewing, reflecting and learning many of the lessons from the competitive season. Some will do a superficial review. Some will work hard to tease out the real gems. Often, it's tough to do.

Reviewing your performance can be uncomfortable, especially if you're honest. You may not like some of the things you see. However, when you do honestly review your performance, you will be able to put a plan into place to tackle the things you are not completely happy with. Once you have done that, your training program starts to write itself. Even better, you know that the time you are spending in training will directly help improve your game. It might surprise you to know that a lot of very high-profile (and highly paid) professional athletes do training sessions, or play matches, without really knowing what they are trying to achieve. As a result, they are missing the opportunity to squeeze every ounce of benefit from that session, and missing opportunities to improve. The truly world-class athletes know exactly how each session will help them become better.

There tends to be a close link between reviewing your performances and developing long-term focus. It is very difficult to have clear, long-term focus if you're not really sure what you are working on. It is tough to keep focused on training for a long period if you are not sure how each session and each match is helping to make you a better player.

You will probably also see how this all links to confidence:

- Imagine the difference in your confidence going into a tough tournament if you know your training has been incredibly focused.
- Imagine how much more confident you will feel if you know that you have been getting better and better week by week. How will you feel when you know you have almost eliminated some of the weakest areas in your game?
- Imagine how you'd feel if your previously shaky technique was now rock solid because you've been working on it and testing it for months.

Learning can be uncomfortable for us because inevitably it means making mistakes[19]. If we only attempt things which we are comfortable with, we will never progress[20]. Learning does not happen in the comfort zone, it happens in the 'discomfort zone'. We have to push our boundaries. As human beings, we are fantastic learners. We are wired up for learning. Often, we shut down our innate abilities to learn because we get scared to make mistakes or are scared to fail.

If you want to become an awesome learner again, go back to the basics. Remember how you learned to walk. You stood up and fell over. You fell over a lot! As a baby you kept getting up and falling over. Each time, you would refine it very slightly and then try again. You never gave up. You had no fear of mistakes. Instead, you kept going and eventually succeeded. If you apply this to your sports performance and even your life, you might be surprised at what you can achieve.

Pushing the Envelope and Loving your Discomfort Zone

In Stage Three, we used some insights from world-class performers, to help us understand how to develop Mental Toughness. Let's take another glimpse into the worlds of:

- Kenny Atkinson: Multiple Michelin Starred Chef
- Chris Cook: Double Olympian
- Alison Waters: World Number 3 Squash Player
- Bruce Duncan: World-Leading Adventure Racer
- Andy McMenemy: World-Record Breaking Ultra Distance Runner
- Ben Saunders: Record-Breaking Polar Explorer

Take A Step into The Unknown

When we push our limits, we enter virgin territory. We take on challenges we've not encountered before. Our own life experience will tell us that there can be a multitude of demands that we've not experienced and questions that we've never answered. As we push ourselves, and leave our familiar territory, the challenges can become uncomfortable and demand more of us. Polar explorer, Ben Saunders knows that world record breaking attempts inevitably require him, and his team, to take on an array of challenges that they have never encountered:

"I really push the limits when I set the bar. It starts in the planning. In 2004, at the age of 26, I set out to cross the Arctic Ocean, from Russia to Canada. At the time there were panels of experts saying that it couldn't be done. Fortunately, no one told me. In 2012 we're planning to do a four month, 1,800-mile expedition from the coast of Antarctica to the South Pole and back on foot. It's the first time anyone will have completed it unsupported. When you set the bar that high, everything else scales up; the training, the funding, the number of complications. Therefore, you push the boundaries with everything. We're starting to prepare for the South Pole now. As a team we are going to the Isle of Skye, into the wilderness. We need to build the relationships because the human dynamic will be tested more than ever. When we get to Antarctica, once we get started, giving up will not be an option. It's a £1.4 million expedition. We have one shot."

We Need to Be Prepared To Fail

Inevitably, when we pushing our boundaries, we will experience failure. Back in 2012, Kenny Atkinson had been awarded two Michelin stars and was working on a third. Many people would imagine that he was past the point where he failed, or made mistakes. However, the reality is significantly different.

Kenny Atkinson:

"For new dishes it can take 10 or more attempts. Sometimes we will end up just scrapping it. Other times we might get it right first time, but it's quite rare."

There is a popular misconception that world class people make few mistakes and that they tend to get things right first time. Olympic swimmer Chris Cook spent years trying to perfect elements of his race. Here is an excerpt from a presentation that Chris and I delivered:

"Simon: I remember your first GB (Great Britain) cap in Dublin, when you came eighth in the European Championships. You were really disappointed with the performance and especially with your start. I can remember sitting with yourself and Jock (the coach) in that tiny office behind the pool, watching the video of the race. We watched your start, which was pretty terrible. You lost several meters on the other competitors. But that was the spark that drove us for years to work on your start. Over the course of the next six years, we took a few tenths of a second out of that start. For me, that still has an impact. Most people would say that working for years to take a few tenths of a second off of a start is a long time. We brought in the physiologists, the bio-mechanist and performance analyst, just to take a few tenths off of the start. And then you're going to do the same on your first length, and then on your turn, and then on your return length and the finish. They are the tiny details that take hours to get right, hours and hours. All of that started because you got to the European Championships and failed.

Chris: Yes, every time I was confronted by a failure, or I didn't quite hit that target, I just viewed it as a bunch of opportunities. It was a chance to take another step forwards. It wasn't quite good enough, but I could find out how to get it good enough."

Failing Is Not Failure

World class performers do not tend to view 'failing' as 'failure'. Olympian Chris Cook describes failures as 'a bunch of opportunities' to improve and develop. In that respect, many of those at the pinnacle of their field understand the value of failures and mistakes. Far from being negative, mistakes are viewed as essential.

Alison Waters understands the value of her mistakes:

"I see mistakes as a positive. Just the other day I did a set of eight exercises that I hadn't done before. I think about half of them felt right, but the other half just didn't feel right. The ones that don't feel right help you to know the difference between feeling right and not. Next time you may only make one or two mistakes in the set. The mistakes help you work out what you need to be doing, so you can work on those little things. You have to have the mistakes to make yourself stronger in a way. If you didn't make mistakes, you wouldn't really learn would you?

If you're making mistakes in your training, you must be outside your comfort zone, which is good. That tells me I am pushing hard enough. If I am not making mistakes, I'm probably not pushing hard enough".

Alison identifies another very important facet. Mistakes help her to know when she's operating outside of her comfort zone. If she's not making mistakes, she's probably not pushing the boundaries. If she's not pushing the boundaries, she's not improving.

World record breaking polar explorer, Ben Saunders, shares that mentality:

"If I know how I'm going to do it, the challenge is not hard enough."

World class people appear to share a common view of mistakes and imperfections. They do not try to forget about them. They are not aiming to get over them. In fact, their approach seems to be the reverse opposite. World class people look for them and actively use their mistakes.

Ouch, That Hurts

Often our greatest challenges, and sometimes our greatest falls, provide us with the most powerful lessons. Undoubtedly, these can hurt. Failures and set-backs are not nice experiences often, but they can be incredibly valuable if we make the most of them.

Bruce Duncan also knows that set-backs can hurt:

"I guess now, I try to learn from mistakes very quickly. I think it's important to get back on the horse and carry on. Sometimes set-backs hurt. They can be painful. I know that, so I prepare myself for that. I know that I will be in some pain and discomfort, but it will be worthwhile."

During his work over the last 20 years, I've noticed that truly great athletes learn from everything: the good, the bad and the average. Ultimately, those who squeeze every last drop of benefit from their experiences tend to be the ones who excel.

Ben Saunders remembers his very first polar expedition:

"We did it on a shoe string. To be honest, it was a complete failure. We didn't get to the pole. I got frost bite, we suffered from hunger, we were attacked by a polar bear. Looking back, we took a bit of a radical approach. It was the first attempt. I was looking at it as an athletic challenge, but I hadn't trained enough, I wasn't prepared, I was inexperienced. There wasn't one big thing that went wrong that caused us to fail, but lots of little things. Looking back, I was young, 23 years old, my metabolic rate was high, so I needed many more calories. My equipment and clothing weren't quite right. Lots of little errors, but I could see how it needed to be improved. There is no textbook in polar exploration.

The experience left me feeling gutted. I felt like it had been a huge failure. I was physically knackered. Financially it had left me with next to nothing. I was convinced that we'd come home as heroes but there was no 'fanfare'. In hindsight though, I'm glad I had the experience."

A lot of people in Ben's position may have concluded that polar exploration was not for them. However, Ben simply used the lessons to ensure that he was successful next time. As I write this, Ben is on his way home from Antarctica. He has just attempted, and failed, in a world-record attempt. I'm pretty sure it'll be another step on his journey to success.

Where Is Our Limit?

As we can see, the challenges that truly extend us, are the ones that help us to take significant steps in our growth and development. Sometimes these challenges are set for us or imposed by circumstance. Sometimes we take them on when they arrive. Sometimes, we might shy away from them. World class people seem to not only take on challenges when they are presented; they actually seek them out. Ultimately, they realize that their limits are dictated by their perception. They know that 'impossible' is simply a word that's used to describe something they haven't yet done.

World-record breaking ultra-distance runner, Andy McMenemy explains how he pushed his own boundaries:

"The limit is always self-imposed. When I first ran a five-kilometer race, I wondered if I could run a 10k. Then I wondered if I could run a marathon. Some people start to ask if they could run a quicker marathon. I started to ask if I could run further; maybe back to back marathons or ultra-marathons? When I did the Marathon de Sables, it was the furthest I'd ever run in a week (151 miles). During Challenge 66, I did my first ever 1000-mile month.

You're crossing uncharted territory all the time. When I did three ultras on the trot I was into new territory. The first week of Challenge 66 was over 200 miles, so new territory. Then I was hitting the new milestones with almost every stride. Then doing it all with injuries. All of these experiences pushed me into new territory.

The whole event was like that, the logistics and everything. There were so many times when we thought, 'how the hell are we going to do this?'"

Relish the Unknown

Mentally Tough people take uncertainty, set-backs and challenges in their stride. They seem to have a different perspective on these experiences. So, how do world class people view uncertainty? Here are some of the observations I've made over the years.

- Uncertainty is normal: To world class people, uncertainty is normal. Unlike the majority of us, the very best in the world deliberately seek out uncertainty. They push themselves way beyond their comfort zone. They are always seeking to explore new territory, try new things and go beyond that which has been done before. As such, they are continually surrounded by uncertainty.

- Uncertainty provides opportunities: Creativity actually requires uncertainty. It requires us to move away from what we know. To be creative, and to innovate, we need to break the mold and abandon our familiar territory. Scientists often do this when they disprove theories. They discard what they know (and often what they have built their reputations on) and enter a state of limbo, a state of 'not knowing'.

- Uncertainty breeds creativity: Leading business realize that the state of uncertainty is a key part of the creative process. Leading businesses often do the same. They know that when they innovate to create a competitive advantage, that advantage is only temporary. It is lost almost immediately. Almost as soon as they have changed (and created some certainty), they have to change again. In doing so, they dive back into uncertainty.

- Uncertainty is exciting: Uncertainty is the reason why people watch sports. If we know the outcome, the spectacle loses its magic. Uncertainty presents us with challenges. It stretches us. Ultimately of course, it helps us to become better at what we do. The experience of taking on challenges actually drives world class people and motivates them. They enjoy it!

So what is it that allows world class people to continually and deliberately dive into uncertainty? One answer is; courage. Psychologist Rollo May[21], understands that uncertainty is often accompanied by anxiety. In psychology, hardiness, is said to provide us with the courage to pursue the future, despite its uncertainty.

So, what gives rise to this courage? World class people will take a leap of faith, a leap into the unknown. They have the courage to jump, not knowing where they will land. They are happy to land wherever they land. World class people continually push themselves beyond their own limits. Their experiences tell them that when they do push themselves beyond the limit of what they previously thought was possible they come out on the other side.

Attempting something means taking on a challenge. To world class people, taking on the challenge is the point. The attempt is the prize. The outcome is less important. If we take on a challenge and do not succeed, have we failed? If we never attempted the challenge, what have we gained?

According to Ambrose Redmoon[1]:

"Courage is not the absence of fear, but rather the judgment that something else is more important than fear."

In reality, the future is always uncertain, no matter how much certainty we think it may have. In that case, we simply have to choose how we perceive it and respond to it.

How do you approach uncertainty? Do you adopt the 'bring it on' mind-set or the 'make it go away' mind-set? That choice is yours.

What Can We Learn?

The accounts from our world class people are incredibly revealing. They are not afraid to push their boundaries and work outside of their comfort zone[22]. They know that they are likely to fail. They understand that they will invariably make many attempts before they get it right. Sometimes it will take literally hundreds of hours of work, years of practice. Unlike many people, they embrace the opportunities.

I once asked polar explorer Ben Saunders what he felt his biggest lesson had been, to date. The response was telling:

"Not being afraid to set big goals. If I know how I'm going to do it, the challenge is not hard enough. Not to be afraid of failure. I have failed far more times than I have succeeded."

Coaches Workshop on Critical Standards

England Squash was one of the most successful sporting organizations on the planet. They dominated their sport for around 20 years. As you might imagine, they didn't take like losing. So, they tore up the floor boards when they came second in the World Championships, to find our why they'd lost. Like many other successful individuals and organizations, they understand the importance of getting the fine details right. They are proactively self-critical and constantly looking for ways to improve. This process of continually critiquing standards, and working to improve them, helps to drive individuals and teams towards success.

Here are some of the Key Messages from England Squash:

- Even those at the top of the world constantly keep pushing. Yesterday's competitive advantage may not be today's and is unlikely to be tomorrow's.

- They continually question what they do and how to do it. They are always looking for ways to get better.

- England Squash take coaches out of their comfort zone and challenge them to become better.

- They foster the same habits in the players, by ensuring that everyone adopts them from the very top downwards.

- They constantly dare to be better.

- Excellence is created because they challenge themselves and each other. They create discomfort through 'brutal honesty', demanding ever greater attention to detail and by asking the tough questions.

How did England Squash respond to being the runner up?

Would your team respond the same way?

So, how do you develop the same mind-set within your team?

Here are some questions to get you started:

1. Which areas of your team's performance are most crucial? What are the five most important things that you need to get right?

✓   In Stage Two, we asked what your 'Two Lengths of the Pool' and 'Five Keys' were. These are often good starting points.

2. Score each of these on a scale of 1-10 (10 = perfect every single time)

3. What do you need to do, as a team, to improve the scores by just one point in each area?

✓   What are the details that you need to improve and how can you improve them?

4. What differences will you notice when the scores have increased by just one point?

✓   What will you see and hear? How will the players be thinking and behaving?

5. As a coach, how can you challenge your players to 'raise their game' and boost the scores by one point?

Key	Score	To increase by one point, we need to...	When we've increased by one point, I'll notice...	I can challenge my players by...

Once you have increased by one point, it's time to re-assess. How do you get another one-point increase? It's a very simple, but very powerful process if you keep doing it!

The greatest performers are never content. They have a very healthy dissatisfaction with their performance because they know there is always something to work on. When I ask junior athletes to rate their performance on a scale of 1-10, many will say eight or nine. When I ask a world champion, they often say four!

Does that mean the junior athlete is better than the world champion, or simply that the world champion has a greater appreciation of the improvements they can still make?

Great individuals and organizations realize that their discomfort is temporary. By stepping into their Discomfort Zone, they eventually become comfortable with whatever it was that caused the discomfort. Essentially, their Comfort Zone grows to encompass all the things they were not comfortable with. As they begin to feel comfortable, they step into discomfort again...and so, they go on.

Where Is Your Discomfort Zone?

- What currently makes you feel uncomfortable?
- Which things do you tend to avoid rather than approach?
- When do you tend to feel out of your depth?
- Does criticism make you uncomfortable?
- What if you were challenges to be more precise, execute a skill more accurately, or with less time?
- What if you were challenged to maintain a high standard for a longer period?
- Are there specific skills that you find more difficult, or situations that present a tougher challenge?

When you start to answer some of these questions, you begin to appreciate where your Comfort Zone ends and your Discomfort Zone begins. For example, when you read the title of this workshop, did you think, "why are you asking me? I thought this was supposed to be about the players." Did you think, "I'd rather not answer these questions about myself", or "maybe I'll skip this section"? Would answering these questions take you into your Discomfort Zone?

The reason to ask you is pretty simple. If you can't do it, you'll find it very hard to get the players to do it.

Keir Worth explains that the entire organization needs to be able to step into the Discomfort Zone. It trickles down from the top. As the person who heads up High Performance, it starts with him. He needs to set the tone for the Coaches, who then influence the players.

So, where does your Comfort Zone end, and your Discomfort Zone begin?
When do you start to become uncomfortable?
Use these little tools to help you.

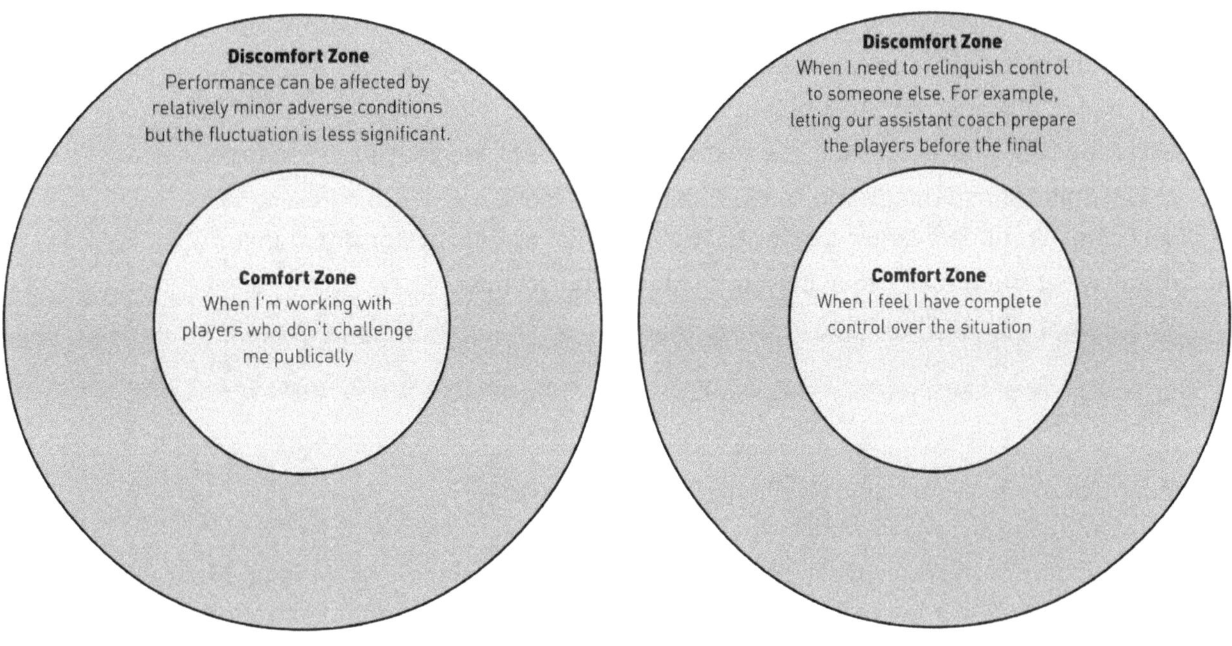

The next question is...
How can you step into your Discomfort Zone and learn how to become comfortable with it?

Summarizing Stage Four

You're just one stage away from becoming a Mental Toughness Master!

Now that you've completed Stage Four, you will understand...

1. How the world's greatest sports organizations and individuals stay ahead by continually pushing themselves into their Discomfort Zone:
- ✓   With 'brutal honesty'.
- ✓   By asking the tough questions
2. The importance of pushing, making mistakes and using them to get better!
- ✓   'Failures' do not equal 'Failure'
- ✓   If I'm making mistakes, it means I'm out of my comfort zone
3. How world class performers approach uncertainty, set-backs and challenges:
- ✓   Uncertainty is normal, provides opportunities and is exciting
- ✓   Set-backs are opportunities to learn!
4. How to identify your Discomfort Zone and use it to improve your performance:
- ✓   Understand those things you tend to back-away from
5. How to use an understanding of 'critical standards' to improve performance:
- ✓   Know what the most critical elements of your performance are.
- ✓   Know what you need to do to improve them.

The Next Step...

Stage 5 – Toughness; Tenacity, Resilience and Composure.

With the strong foundation from the first four stages in place, the Master Mental Toughness program will examine how world class performers develop the toughness to venture where others do not dare. We will explore the principles and methods that are used by world class athletes, adventurers and special-forces personnel. By learning from world class performers, we gain a unique insight and understanding into how they became so tough, and what allows them to push as hard as they do. We can then apply this knowledge to fostering these attributes in our own players.

This is it.

Are you ready to push to the summit?

STAGE FIVE: TOUGHNESS – TENACITY, RESILIENCE AND COMPOSURE

The final section will allow us to cover the following key issues:

1. Going where others have not gone before
2. Principles and practices of world athletes
3. Learning from adventurers
4. Lessons from the special-forces personnel
5. Fostering resilient qualities among players
6. Deconstruction of Pressure
7. Composure
8. Being world class in everything you do

Welcome to Stage Five – Toughness: Tenacity, Resilience and Composure

Welcome to Stage Five. By this point you will know what Mental Toughness is, what it looks like and how to recognize it. You'll have some ways of assessing Mental Toughness (such as *The Mental Toughness Matrix*). During Stage Two, you will have learned some practical strategies to consistently engineer an optimal mind-set. This will help you to achieve your best performances consistently. Stage Three will have taught you how to develop accountability and responsibility in your players. Through Stage Four you will have discovered the importance of stepping into the Discomfort Zone. With these in place, we can put the final pieces of the jigsaw into place.

Stage 1 – Understand Mental Toughness (Complete)

Stage 2 – Consistent Optimal Performance (Complete)

Stage 3 – Accountability and Responsibility (Complete)

Stage 4 – Enter the Discomfort Zone (Complete)

Stage 5 – Toughness: Tenacity, Resilience and Composure (You are Here)

A Solid Foundation

By this point, much of the work has been done. When we understand what Mental Toughness looks like, sounds like, thinks like and acts like, we can start encouraging players to become tougher. When we have a solid mental game, we're able to consistently perform at our best. That is an important part of Mental Toughness. Simply by being focused, confident and motivated consistently, we become mentally stronger.

By becoming accountable and responsible, we are able to take control and ensure that we learn from everything. This helps us to make the most of our experiences and bounce-back from set-backs stronger. As a result, we're also more willing to enter ourselves into our Discomfort Zone and start to push our limits. These are the characteristics that come together to form Mental Toughness.

Why Is This Stage So Important?

During this final stage, we will look at how to help players display composure, resilience and tenacity when they face the most demanding challenges. In particular, we will look at the concept of pressure. We will identify strategies that can help players to perform at their peak in any situation. In addition, we'll look at how some of the toughest athletes in the world develop Mental Toughness in themselves and their teams.

This is the icing on the cake!

During this stage, you will learn:

1. How the help your players become composed, so that they can make optimal decisions and execute skills to a high level in any situation.
2. How the world's toughest athletes respond to demanding challenges.
3. The importance of solid focus, confidence and motivation.
4. How world class performers become resilient and tenacious.
5. How to apply all of these lessons and strategies to yourself, your players and your team.

Use these tools to help you develop Composure, Tenacity and Resilience.

Let's do it!

Mental Toughness in Action

Right at the start of Master Mental Toughness, we identified the key elements that we see in mentally tough athletes. Players with mental strength will push themselves to their limits and thrive in adverse conditions. Those players also tend to take on the most demanding challenges, rather than back away. They will take responsibility for their performance and use criticism to get better. In demanding situations, mentally tough players will tend to be composed. They make better decisions and execute skills to a consistently high standard.

Can you remember the six signs of Mental Toughness?

Athletes who consistently perform at their best in adverse conditions:
Mentally tough athletes tend to be focused, confident and motivated, whatever the situation. Every athlete experiences their peaks and troughs, whether that is through injury, lack of form, de-selection, a run of poor results, or whatever. Every athlete has been in situations where the chips are down and they have their backs to the wall. Mentally tough athletes tend to apply themselves consistently, whether they are on a high, or at the bottom of the deepest low. I often say to athletes, "I want to know what you're like on the shitty days".

Athletes who come back stronger from set-backs
Athletes with mental strength tend to display bounce-back ability. I have come to realize that great athletes seem to experience the same amount of good luck and bad luck as everyone else. However, their response to their luck is normally different. When they experience set-backs, mentally tough athletes knuckle down, apply themselves, learn as much as they possibly can from the experience and grow from it.
http://www.be-world-class.com/sport/learn-from-everything-544

Athletes who are composed in pressurized situations
When athletes perceive that they are under pressure, some will panic. Sometimes the game plan flies out of the window and they start to make strange decisions and unforced errors. Mentally tough athletes, however, tend to have the ability to remain composed. They tend not to panic, they stay on task, keep focused and stick to the game plan. When they make mistakes, they simply focus back onto the task in hand and execute their skills.

Athletes who actively seek out, and thrive in, their Discomfort Zone
Some athletes will respond well if they are pushed outside of their comfort zones. Truly great athletes go a step further. They actively seek out opportunities to push themselves into their discomfort zone. The world class athletes that I've worked with will say that the alarm bells start ringing when they become comfortable. These people relish the challenge and go looking for it!

Athletes who push to their limit, not just the point of discomfort
Most people stop when things become uncomfortable.

Although we think of this in a physical sense (i.e. the point we become tired or feel physical pain), this concept extends to other limits too. Some people give up when they've tried a new skill a few times and it's not worked perfectly. They don't like the feeling of failing because it is uncomfortable. Other people keep going and keep failing, until they get it right. They don't stop at the point where it becomes uncomfortable; they stop when they hit their limit.

Athletes who are self-critical and seek critical feedback from others
Some athletes are uncomfortable with criticism. Others will listen, take criticism on board and acknowledge it. The better athletes will recognize that it is a gift and use it to its fullest extent. The world class athletes that I've met actually seek out critical feedback and then squeeze every possible ounce of benefit from it. To them, critical feedback is like oxygen. It fuels their development. Without it, they know they cannot grow.

When we look at the clues, it's possible to see the three critical components of Mental Toughness;

Composure
Resilience
Tenacity

What do these three words mean?

Composure

The ability to consistently make optimal decisions and to execute skills to a high standard, whatever the situation.

Resilience

The ability to bounce-back from set-backs and to thrive in adversity.

Tenacity

The ability to push to the limit and refuse to quit.

So, how do we develop these three critical elements?

Composure

In order to make optimal decisions and execute skills to a high standard, we need to focus! When performance deteriorates, it is often because we're simply not focused on the right thing at the right time. The truth is, we are always focused on something. The question is, are we focused on the most effective thing in each moment? If we're worried about missing a hit, we will not be 100% focused on watching the ball and we're likely to not to strike the ball as well as we could.

In Stage Two, we learned how to hone focus. Focus is fundamental to composure. In a sense, composure is simply the ability to focus in more demanding situations. If you cannot focus effectively, you'll find it really tough to do when the challenge increases.

So, how can we help players to remain composed in critical moments?

Here's an article that I wrote a few years ago, which gives some valuable insights.

Pressure…What Pressure?
Simon Hartley
Be World Class

"Pressure is a word that is misused in our vocabulary. When you start thinking of pressure, it's because you've started to think of failure."
Tommy Lasorda, LA Dodgers Coach.

There is no such thing as pressure.

It is one of the great secrets in sport psychology that even the professionals often get wrong. Most sport psychologists and coaches talk about managing pressure, which makes the mistake of assuming that it exists. It doesn't exist, so managing it is a non-sense. In fact, by trying to manage it, we start to believe it might be real.

"Pressure is nothing more than the shadow of great opportunity." Michael Johnson.

Let's start with the basics. People create pressure for themselves (Beilock, 2010). The only way we can ever experience pressure is to create it in our own minds. It is a product of our imagination. If we experience pressure it is because we are projecting an imaginary view of the future (Markman, et al 2008). Normally we feel pressure when we perceive that there is an expectation on us. Like pressure, expectations are also figments of our imagination. They are also imaginary projections into the future. Any view of the future must be produced in our imagination, there is no-where else it can come from (Markman, et al 2008). Therefore, expectations are normally a product of your imagination or someone else's. Either way, expectations are not real. Normally, we feel pressure when we start imagining what might happen if we don't achieve the outcome we desire or that we expect. "What if I don't win?" "What will the media say?" "What will the coach say?"… "What will people think?"

Some teams and individuals habitually under-perform when they reach major world events. The reason for this may well be because the athletes feel pressure to perform for their nation (Gerrard, 2010). For example, when athletes compete for their country, in their national sport, there is normally a lot of media hype. This is true in New Zealand for the All Blacks Rugby Team (Huw, 2010) and true in England for the England Football Team. In the 2010 FIFA World Cup, England performed well below par. There were several possible reasons given for the performances. On a number of occasions, Fabio Capello sighted "fear" and "pressure" (Christenson, 2010). Many people would logically deduce that this was linked closely to the media coverage and the hype that had been created in the lead up to the event. However, the media coverage and the hype will only be perceived as pressure, if players buy into it. Just like any other expectation, it's born out of the imagination. In this case, it was the imaginations of the journalists, the public, The Football Association, the sponsors and possibly even the players and staff of Team England.

By projecting an image of what might happen, we may start doubting the outcome and feeling uneasy. We need to recognize that our imagination is incredibly powerful. Used positively, it can help us to optimize our performance. However, we have to be aware that we also use our imagination to create trap-doors for ourselves. The simple principle is that we should only concern ourselves with reality, not fantasy. Fantasy is a product of our imagination, just as expectations and pressure are. Often people have hopes for us, which they express. We sometimes take those on board as expectations, which we then try to fulfill. If we buy into expectations, we are trying to live up to a fantasy. The best thing to do is to recognize it for what it is and to get on with reality.

Athletes feel pressure when they get the job wrong (Lane, 2001). Typically, athletes think that their job is to win, to climb up the rankings, to secure prize money or sponsorship. However, none of those things are the job. Normally when we get the job wrong, it is because we're too busy focusing on the outcome. In reality, our job is to deliver the process. By aiming for the result, we set ourselves a job which is outside of our control (Bull, 1996). The fact that it is outside of our control means that it's uncertain. Winning is never certain. Hitting a target is never certain. There is always an element of uncertainty. This uncertainty is what tends to cause us the angst (Boelen & Reijntjes, 2009). How can we be completely confident in our ability to achieve something that has uncertainty? If you're trying to do an impossible job or even a job which you have no control over, you will probably imagine pressure because you will not be 100 per cent sure that you can do the job. The job might seem too big or too daunting. If the athlete believes the job is to win the tournament, they might doubt their ability to do it. Even a confident athlete won't know that they can do that job. There is often a gap between what we believe we can achieve, and what we think we must achieve. That gap manifests as the worry and anxiety we associate with pressure. This is illustrated in Csikszentmihalyi's (2008) model of the challenge and skills balance. If we create an expectation for ourselves (or take on board someone else's expectations), we post a target. If we are not absolutely sure that we can achieve that target, we might start to have doubts and worries. If we also give that target some meaning, we will magnify our doubts and worries.

As we've said already, we create pressure therefore we can 'de-construct it' (Hartley, 2011). The easiest way is not to create it in the first place. However, if we do feel pressure, we have the ability to dismantle it and start to see the reality rather than the illusion. If you start to perceive pressure, take a few moments to remind yourself why there is no pressure and never was any pressure. Normally this involves a slight reality check and a quick reminder of the job. Once we do that, we are more likely to be able to focus on exactly what we need to do in that moment (Hartley, 2010). In reality, the job we need to do will normally be pretty simple and something we're very capable of doing. Rather than trying to serve for the match or win Championship point, we'll simply be trying to serve. Instead of trying to win the World Cup, the job is simply to take a penalty kick. Rather than attempting to win the Ryder Cup, the job is simply to execute a three-foot putt (Fisher, 1998).

Once performers have got the hang of de-constructing pressure, I like to start stress-testing it with them to see how robust it is. Like many things, it's easy to ditch pressure in a classroom environment or a training session. It's a greater challenge in the heat of competition. To put it into a practical setting, I often use pressure training exercises (Taylor & Wilson, 2005). To be honest, that is probably a daft name. The aim of pressure training is simple. The performer's task is simply to stick to their simple job, whatever we throw at them. For example, we could introduce prizes, incentives or consequences. Or, we could put players in situations where they have less time and space than expected. We could change the environment or introduce new challenges at a moment's notice.

Why?

Because those are the challenges they face in competition!

References

Beilock, S. (2010) Choke, New York: Free Press.

Boelen, P. A. & Reijntjes, A. (2009) 'Intolerance of uncertainty and social anxiety', Journal of Anxiety Disorders, 23, 130-135

Bull, S. J. (1996) The Mental Game Plan: Getting Psyched for Sport, London: Sport Dynamics.

Christenson, M. (2010) 'World Cup 2010: Capello says pressure hindered England players', The Guardian. 21st June 2010.

Csikszentmihalyi, M. (2008) 'Creativity, fulfillment and flow', Keynote Presentation to TED Conference. 24th October 2008. Online. Available HTTP: <http://www.youtube.com/watch?v=fXIeFJCqsPs> (accessed 15th December 2010)

Fisher, M. (1998) The Golfer and the Millionaire, New York: Cassell Illustrated.

Gerrard, S. (2010) 'England skipper Steven Gerrard tells under-fire stars to make their nation proud ahead of do-or-die showdown with Slovenia', Daily Record. 23rd June 2010. Online. Available HTTP: <http://www.dailyrecord.co.uk/football/world-cup-2010/news/2010/06/23/england-skipper-steven-gerrard-tells-under-fire-stars-to-make-their-nation-proud-ahead-of-do-or-die-showdown-with-slovenia-86908-22353116/> (accessed 15th December 2010)

Fisher, M. (1998) The Golfer and the Millionaire, New York: Cassell Illustrated.

Gerrard, S. (2010) 'England skipper Steven Gerrard tells under-fire stars to make their nation proud ahead of do-or-die showdown with Slovenia', Daily Record. 23rd June 2010. Online. Available HTTP: <http://www.dailyrecord.co.uk/football/world-cup-2010/news/2010/06/23/england-skipper-steven-gerrard-tells-under-fire-stars-to-make-their-nation-proud-ahead-of-do-or-die-showdown-with-slovenia-86908-22353116/> (accessed 15th December 2010)

Hartley, S.R. (2010) 'Athletic Focus & Sport Psychology: Key To Peak Performance', Podium Sports Journal, December 2010. Available Online. HTTP. < http://www.podiumsportsjournal.com/2010/12/09/athletic-focus-sport-psychology-key-to-peak-performance/> (accessed 21st December 2010).

Hartley, S.R. (2011) Peak Performance Every Time, London: Routledge.

Huw, J. (2010) 'Rugby World Cup 2011. Are the All Blacks Peaking Too Soon?', Suite101.com, 2nd August 2010. Online. Available HTTP: < http://www.suite101.com/content/rugby-world-cup-2011--are-the-all-blacks-peaking-too-soon--a268927> (accessed 15th December 2010)

Lane, A. (2001) 'Relationship between perceptions of performance expectations and mood amongst distance runners', Journal of Science and Medicine in Sport, 4(1), 116-128.

Manz, C.C. (2000) Emotional Discipline: The Power to Choose How You Feel, San Francisco: Berrett-Koehler.

Markham, K.D., Klein, W.M.P. and Suhr, J.A (2008) Handbook of Imagination and Mental Simulation, London: Psychology Press.

Taylor, J & Wilson, G.S. (2005) Applying Sport Psychology: Four Perspectives, Champaign, IL: Human Kinetics.

You can use these principles to help your players produce their best performances in 'big matches' or when they are feeling pressure.

Key Messages from Pressure… What Pressure? are:

- Take control of your mind and emotions
- Know that pressure is imaginary. It can only exist in our imagination.
- Know the job and keep it simple.
- Practice being in situations where you have less time and space, so that it becomes familiar.

Resilience

Resilient athletes approach challenges and set-backs by looking for the opportunities. They tend to ask, "how can I?" or "how could I?" rather than "why can't I?"

Here's an example, from my work as a sport psychology coach:

"A few years ago, I worked with a world class Olympic swimmer, who was ranked in the top 10 in the world for his event. He had sustained a back injury that threatened to end his competitive year. His injury meant that he could not swim more than a couple of lengths before succumbing to the pain. Many swimmers would imagine that being unable to swim would be a show stopper.

I chatted with him about the injury for a while. During my career, I have worked with some Paralympic athletes. Whenever I start working with them, I begin by asking them what they can do. Many people might start by asking a disabled athlete what they cannot do, but I've always done the opposite. Therefore, I decided to take the same approach with the injured swimmer.

Through the course of the conversation, we discovered that there were many things that the athlete could still do. In fact, this injury gave him an opportunity to work on a few skills that he rarely had the chance to practice, such as sculling. When sculling, swimmers keep their body rigid and only move the water using their hands and arms. It is a skill that helps them to move water more effectively and therefore to become quicker.

So, together we reworked his training program in order to build upon the things the athlete could do. Once his injury subsided, he found that he was significantly quicker because he'd used the time to work on his skills."

Resilient athletes find a way to come back stronger! They always find a way to learn something or gain something from each experience. They see the opportunities to become better because they are always looking for them.

How can players learn to become more resilient?

Here are some Top Tips:

- Stop judging! If you've decided that a situation is bad, you'll tend so see the threats and it'll be harder to find the opportunities.
- The opportunities that you'll find tend to relate to processes, i.e. you're presented with an opportunity to learn something or improve skills. Therefore, those who are focused on their processes, tend to see the opportunities.
- If you're only motivated by the outcome (or the result), these opportunities are harder to spot.

Tenacity

Tenacious players will push themselves to the limit and won't quit until they've given their last ounce of energy.

"I remember watching my home-town team recently in a Cup match. With around five minutes to go, the opposition scored and took a 2-1 lead. All of a sudden, my team kicked into action. The energy levels and urgency picked up. They ran harder. They were more physical. The full backs started to over-lap. Midfielders started getting into the penalty box and players all over the field made 'heroic' tackles to get the ball back".

Do you think that is tenacity?

Personally, I don't think so. I asked myself why they needed to go behind on the scoreboard before they put their foot on the gas. Why weren't they doing that five minutes earlier? Clearly the players had the energy to do it. Physically they were capable. Obviously, they were not pushing themselves to the limit and giving every last ounce of energy for the whole 90 minutes.

Tenacious players would not wait until they needed to give more. Tenacious players give everything they can anyway.

So, what are the secrets to tenacity?

Key Messages from World-Leading Adventure Racer, Bruce Duncan.

- "If you want something enough, nothing is too much hard work, nothing is too painful"
- Bruce emphasizes that when the "why" is strong enough, we can find the "how".

Of course, motivation is key!

We have to be motivated by the right reason, in order to develop tenacity.

Question: Which is stronger, which is likely to give us the more tenacious players?

- the desire to win
  or
- the desire to play the best possible game?

Some people might say, "the desire to win".
Others might disagree, with very good reason:

- What happens if we're 4-0 down with 10 minutes to go and we don't believe we can win?
- What happens if we're 4-0 up at half time and we think the game's won already?

Do the players display the same degree of tenacity or do they do what my home town team did and only become tenacious when they think there is a need?

The Foundation

Throughout Master Mental Toughness, we have emphasized that each stage of the process provides the foundation for the next stages. Just like building a staircase, each step has to be constructed properly if we want a strong structure.

As we can see:

- Composure is underpinned by Focus and Confidence
- Resilience is also underpinned by Focus (particularly focus on processes) and a desire to learn from everything (which is underpinned by motivation)
- Tenacity is also underpinned by Motivation

Remember, focus follows interest and interest follows what you really care about.

All of this takes us back to a fundamental question.

What's your "why"?

During Stage Two, we learned that Focus, Confidence and Motivation are inter-dependent. They feed off of each other and are built upon each other. We cannot have one without having the other two. When we have all three together, we create a positive spiral of performance. If we're missing one, we tend to find that the other two erode and we end up in a negative spiral.

With these powerful building blocks, you can now start to develop Composure, Resilience and Tenacity in your players!

Coaches Workshop – Building the Mental Toughness Jigsaw

Using what you've learned from world class performers, see if you can apply their thinking to your own challenges.
The question is split into to parts.

1. How have you responded to these challenges in the past?
2. Using what you know about Mental Toughness, how would you respond to these challenges now?

Challenge	How have you responded in the past?	How would you respond now?
You encounter a challenge that you've never come across before.		
You hit rock bottom.		
You fail publicly.		
You are faced with a seemingly impossible challenge.		
You find yourself becoming anxious and feeling under pressure.		

Use the same thought process to help you answer this question:

How can you use what you've learned to help your players respond to the following challenges?

- There's five minutes left on the clock and you are two goals down.
- One of your players is struggling with a potentially career ending injury.
- After 20 minutes, your team is down 3-0.
- Your team goes up 3-0 within half an hour but now find themselves 3-3. There is 10 minutes to go and the opposition are attacking hard.
- Your team is on a five-game losing streak.
- You and your team are being openly criticized.

Those are some hypothetical examples. Your challenge now is to identify the top five challenges that you are experiencing at the moment.

How can you use what you've learned to help your players respond to your current challenges...?

Summarizing Stage Five

Congratulations! You have completed the journey, and have become a Mental Toughness Master!
Now that you've completed Stage Five, you will understand

1. How the help your players become composed, so that they can make optimal decisions and execute skills to a high level in any situation:
✓   Know what to focus on.
✓   Focus on the right things at the right times, whatever the situation.
✓   Know the simple job, and stick to it.
2. How the world's toughest athletes respond to demanding challenges:
✓   They push through the barriers.
3. The importance of solid focus, confidence and motivation:
✓   Focus, confidence and motivation underpin all of the key elements of Mental Toughness: accountability and responsibility,

- the ability to be self-critical and raise standards,

- the ability to enter the Discomfort Zone

- Composure

- Resilience

- Tenacity

4. How world class performers become resilient and tenacious:
✓   Focus on processes and always look for the opportunities to improve them.
✓   Have a rock solid "why" - the right reasons.
5. How to use and apply all of these lessons and strategies to yourself, your players and your team:
✓   You should now have some solid strategies that you can use to help your players and your team to become Mentally Tough.

The next step...

Over to you!

It's time to **DO** it.

As human beings, we learn many things in the same way we learned to walk. Learning to walk requires us to fall over, make mistakes, learn from them and go again.

It's exactly the same with Mental Toughness.

If at first you don't succeed, change and try again... then change and try again... then change and try again.

Remember...

"Giving up is not the result of failure, it is the cause".

CONCLUSION: Key Lessons

Let us close this book by thinking about a few things. The onus is now on you to answer these questions. Give at least five answers to each and make them as detailed as you can because you are now an expert on developing mental toughness:

1. What you have learned about mental toughness?
2. What has changed in your perspective?
3. What you are going to do as a result of reading this book?

Start Coaching and Playing Sports with Confidence and Mental Toughness Today!

Bibliography and Useful Links

[1] Hartley, S.R. (2012) How To Shine; Insights Into Unlocking Your Potential From Proven Winners, London: Capstone.

[2] Sheard, M. (2012) Mental Toughness: The Mind-set Behind Sporting Achievement (2nd Edition), London: Routledge.

[3] Hammermeister, J,. Pickering, M, and Lennox, A. (2011) Military Applications of Performance Psychology Methods and Techniques: An Overview of Practice and Research, Journal of Performance Psychology, 3, 3-13

[4] Ankersen, R. (2011) The Gold Mine Effect; Unlocking The Essence of World Class Performance, London: Rasmus Ankersen.
[5] Donnelly, J.H. and Ivancevich, J.M. (1975) 'Role Clarity and the Salesman', Journal of Marketing, 39(1), 71-74.
[6] Baumeister, R.F. and Showers, C.J. (1986) 'A review of paradoxical performance effects: Choking under pressure in sports and mental tests', European Journal of Social Psychology, 16(4), 361-383
[7] Lindsley, D.H., Brass, D.J. and Thomas, J.B. (1995) 'Efficacy-Performance Spirals: A Multilevel Perspective', Academy of Management Review, 20(3), 645-678.
[8] Bray, S.R. and Brawley, L.R. (2002a) 'Role Efficacy, Role Clarity and Role Performance Effectiveness', Small Group Research, 33(2), 233-253

[9] Bray, S.R. and Brawley, L.R. (2002b) 'Efficacy for Independent Role Functions: Evidence from the Sport Domain, Small Group Research, 33(6), 644-666.
[10] Kloosterman, P. (1988) 'Self Confidence and Motivation in Mathematics', Journal of Educational Psychology, 80(3), 345-351
[11] Bandura, A. (1997) Self-efficacy: The exercise of control, New York: Worth Publishers.
[12] Horn, T. (2008) Advances in Sport Psychology, Champaign, IL: Human Kinetics.
[13] Key, A. (2006) 'Knowing Your Role In Rugby', Rugby Football Union Technical Journal. 1-6.
[14] Frankl, V. E. (2004). Man's search for meaning, London: Rider.

[15] Jauncey, P. (2002) Managing Yourself & Others, Brisbane: CopyRight Publishing.

[16] Hartley, S.R. (2011) Peak Performance Every Time, London: Routledge.
[17] Halden-Brown, S. (2003) Mistakes Worth Making: How to turn sports errors into athletic excellence, Champaign, IL: Human Kinetics.

[18] Orlick, T. (2000) In Pursuit of Excellence: How to Win in Sport and Life Through Mental Training (3rd Edition), Champaign, IL: Human Kinetics.

[19] Colvin, G. (2008) Talent is Overrated: What Really Separates World Class Performers From Everybody Else, New York: Portfolio.

[20] Cotterill, S. and Johnson, P. (2008) 'Exploring the Concept of the Comfort Zone in Professional Soccer Players', Association for Applied Sport Psychology Annual Conference. St Louis, USA

[21] May, R. (1975) The Courage to Create, New York: W.W.Norton.

[22] White, A. A. K. (2009) From Comfort Zone to Performance Management, New York: White & MacLean Publishing.

References

Ankersen, R. (2011) The Gold Mine Effect; Unlocking The Essence of World Class Performance, London: Rasmus Ankersen.

Be World Class Conference (2011) 'Bruce Duncan...on Mental Toughness', 6th October 2011. Online. Available HTTP: http://www.beworldclass.tv (accessed 31st January 2012).

Beilock, S. (2010) Choke, New York: Free Press.

Boelen, P. A. & Reijntjes, A. (2009) 'Intolerance of uncertainty and social anxiety', Journal of Anxiety Disorders, 23, 130-135

Bull, S. J. (1996) The Mental Game Plan: Getting Psyched for Sport, London: Sport Dynamics.

Christenson, M. (2010) 'World Cup 2010: Capello says pressure hindered England players', The Guardian. 21st June 2010.

Colvin, G. (2008) Talent is Overrated: What Really Separates World Class Performers From Everybody Else, New York: Portfolio.

Cotterill, S. and Johnson, P. (2008) 'Exploring the Concept of the Comfort Zone in Professional Soccer Players', Association for Applied Sport Psychology Annual Conference. St Louis, USA

Csikszentmihalyi, M. (2008) 'Creativity, fulfillment and flow', Keynote Presentation to TED Conference. 24th October 2008. Online. Available HTTP: ←http://www.youtube.com/watch?v=fXIeFJCqsPs→ (accessed 15th December 2010)

Engh, F., 2015. The Coach Who Became 'Best Man'. [Online]
Available at: http://www.huffingtonpost.com/fred-engh/the-coach-who-became-best_b_8216402.html
[Accessed 18th October 2015].

Fisher, M. (1998) The Golfer and the Millionaire, New York: Cassell Illustrated.

Frankl, V. E. (2004). Man's search for meaning, London: Rider.

Gerrard, S. (2010) 'England skipper Steven Gerrard tells under-fire stars to make their nation proud ahead of do-or-die showdown with Slovenia', Daily Record. 23rd June 2010. Online. Available HTTP: ←http://www.dailyrecord.co.uk/football/world-cup-2010/news/2010/06/23/england-skipper-steven-gerrard-tells-under-fire-stars-to-make-their-nation-proud-ahead-of-do-or-die-showdown-with-slovenia-86908-22353116/→ (accessed 15th December 2010)

Halden-Brown, S. (2003) Mistakes Worth Making: How to turn sports errors into athletic excellence, Champaign, IL: Human Kinetics.

Hammermeister, J,. Pickering, M, and Lennox, A. (2011) Military Applications of Performance Psychology Methods and Techniques: An Overview of Practice and Research, Journal of Performance Psychology, 3, 3-13

Hartley, S.R. (2010) 'Athletic Focus & Sport Psychology: Key To Peak Performance', Podium Sports Journal, December 2010. Available Online. HTTP. ← http://www.podiumsportsjournal.com/2010/12/09/athletic-focus-sport-psychology-key-to-peak-performance/→ (accessed 21st December 2010).

Hartley, S.R. (2010) 'Learn From Everything', Squash Player, 38(6), 24.

Hartley, S.R. (2011) Peak Performance Every Time, London: Routledge.

Hartley, S.R. (2012) How To Shine; Insights Into Unlocking Your Potential From Proven Winners, London: Capstone.

Heath, R. (2009) Celebrating Failure: The Power of Taking Risks, Making Mistakes and Thinking Big, New Jersey: Career Press.

Huw, J. (2010) 'Rugby World Cup 2011. Are the All Blacks Peaking Too Soon?', Suite101.com, 2nd August 2010. Online. Available HTTP: ← http://www.suite101.com/content/rugby-world-cup-2011--are-the-all-blacks-peaking-too-soon--a268927→ (accessed 15th December 2010)

Jauncey, P. (2002) Managing Yourself & Others, Brisbane: CopyRight Publishing.

Johnson, S. R. et al., 2011. A Coach's Responsibility: Learning How to Prepare Athletes for Peak Performance. The Sport Journal.

Jones, G., Hanton, S., & Connaughton, D. (2002). What is this thing called Mental Toughness? An investigation with elite performers. Journal of Applied Sport Psychology, 14, 211-224.

Jones, G., Hanton, S., & Connaughton, D. (2007). A framework of Mental Toughness in the world's best performers. The Sport Psychologist, 21, 243 – 264.

Jowett, S. & Cockerill, I., 2003. Olympic medallists' perspective of the althlete–coach relationship. Psychology of sport and exercise, 4(4), pp. 313-331.

King, J., 2011. Four Pillars of Destiny: A Guide to Relationships. Bloomington (IN): iUniverse.

Kirousis, W., 2015. Train your best today usac. [Online]
Available at: http://www.slideshare.net/willkirousis/train-your-best-today-usac-51120260
[Accessed 18th October 2015].

Lane, A. (2001) 'Relationship between perceptions of performance expectations and mood amongst distance runners', Journal of Science and Medicine in Sport, 4(1), 116-128.

Lyle, J., 2002. Sports Coaching Concepts: A Framework for Coaches' Behaviour. New York: Psychology Press.
Manz, C.C. (2000) Emotional Discipline: The Power to Choose How You Feel, San Francisco: Berrett-Koehler.

Markham, K.D., Klein, W.M.P. and Suhr, J.A (2008) Handbook of Imagination and Mental Simulation, London: Psychology Press.

May, R. (1975) The Courage to Create, New York: W.W.Norton.

Nicholls, A. R. & Jones, L., 2013. Psychology in Sports Coaching: Theory and Practice. London: Routledge.
Oliver, C., 2015. The Philosophy of a Coach. [Online]
Available at: http://www.slideshare.net/ChrisOliver6/the-philosophy-of-a-coach
[Accessed 18th October 2015].

Orlick, T. (2000) In Pursuit of Excellence: How to Win in Sport and Life Through Mental Training (3rd Edition), Champaign, IL: Human Kinetics.

Pavlov, I., 1960. Conditional Reflexes. New York: Dover Publications.

Pill, S., 2008. Teaching games for understanding. Physical Education and Recreation, 29(2).

Potrac, P., Gilbert, W. & Deninson, J., 2013. Routledge Handbook of Sports Coaching. New York: Routledge.

Rotter, J. B., 1966. Generalized expectancies for internal versus external control of reinforcement. Psychological Monographs: General & Applied, 80(1), pp. 1-28.

Samah, A. et al., 2013. Influence of coaches' behavior on athletes' motivation : Malaysian sport archery experience. International Journal of Research in Management, 5(3), pp. 136-142.

Sheard, M. (2012) Mental Toughness: The Mind-set Behind Sporting Achievement (2nd Edition), London: Routledge.

Stafford, I., 2011. Coaching Children in Sport. London: Taylor & Francis.

Taylor, J & Wilson, G.S. (2005) Applying Sport Psychology: Four Perspectives, Champaign, IL: Human Kinetics.

White, A. A. K. (2009) From Comfort Zone to Performance Management, New York: White & MacLean Publishing.

ABOUT THE AUTHORS

Simon Hartley, MSc.

Simon Hartley is a globally respected sport psychology consultant and performance coach. He helps athletes and business people throughout the world to get their mental game right. For over 20 years, he has worked with gold medalists, world record holders, world champions, top five world ranked professional athletes, and multiple-championship winning teams.

Simon has worked at the highest level of sport, including spells in Premiership football, Premiership rugby union, First Class County Cricket, Super League, golf, tennis, motor sport and with Great British Olympians.

Since 2005, Simon has also applied the principles of sport psychology to business, education, healthcare and the charity sector. This has included projects with some of the world's leading corporations and foremost executives. More recently, Simon has also become a highly acclaimed author and international professional speaker.

For more information, please visit www.be-world-class.com

To find Simon's other books, please visit www.amazon.co.uk/Simon-Hartley/e/B005CERCJQ/

Darren Laver

Darren is one of the most unique and creative coaches in the world. He is the Founder, of the International Street Soccer Association (ISSA), the world-wide recognized street soccer concept, and the Virtual DOC, a soccer club consultancy organization based in America. Darren is also a globally recognized expert Coach and Exhibition Performer. Darren has "dedicated his life" to coaching players to improve their creative skill. He provides training programs, expert advice, coach education as well as running Street Soccer Events for amateur and professional clubs, councils and communities across the world. Darren's influence has grown to be a near global phenomenon.

Darren is a recognized authority on the subject, and his knowledge, performances and exhibitions have allowed coaches, teachers and those involved in the biggest sport in the world seek a more creative, efficient and dynamic way to coach the beautiful game. Darren also works as a 'Coach Educator' and 'Technical Consultant' for the Tennessee State Soccer Association. Darren is recognized as one of the leading Street Soccer coaches and soccer skill performers in the world. Darren's extraordinary abilities and performances led him to being voted one of the best street soccer players in the United Kingdom and was the selected to be 1 of 45 star players to feature in EA Sports FIFA Street (2012 Video Game).

For more information visit www.thevdoc.com